IN THE THICK OF IT

THE LIFE AND TIMES OF C. BEN JOHNSON

In the Thick of It

The Life and Times of C. Ben Johnson

*When Lincoln issued his call for soldiers in 1861,
14-year-old Ben Johnson
"was one of the first to respond,"
joining the Union war effort as a
'musician.'*

William D. Turner

SNOWMASS VILLAGE, COLORADO

In the Thick of It | *The Life and Times of C. Ben Johnson*
By William Dow Turner

Copyright © 2023 by William D. Turner

NOTICE OF RIGHTS
*All rights reserved. No part of this book may be reproduced
or transmitted in any form or by any means, electronic or mechanical,
including photocopying, recording, or by any information storage and retrieval system, without permission in writing from the publisher.*

ISBN: 978-1-7376436-8-5

DESIGN & MAPS | CURT CARPENTER © 2023

PRINTED IN THE UNITED STATES

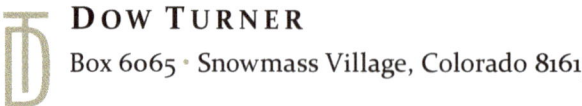

Dow Turner
Box 6065 · Snowmass Village, Colorado 81615

CONTENTS

Author's Note	ix
Acknowledgments	xiii

PART ONE
Early Days, Hard Times, and the Call to War

A Nascent USA	1
Pennsylvania	3
Philadelphia	4
Lincoln, War of the States, and Raising an Army	4
Enter C. Ben Johnson	7
An Off Ramp and an On Ramp	7
A 'Musician' at War	8
Becoming a Scribe	11

PART TWO
Surviving Four Years of War | 15

The Adventures of Ben and the 104th	16
The Peninsular Campaign of 1862	19
The Siege of Charlestown of 1863-64	26
The Shenandoah Valley Campaign of 1864-65	29
Memorial Day and Grand Army of the Republic	31

PART THREE
Pursuing Journalism and Many Causes | 38

Writing About Coal and Workers	38
The Rise of Anthracite Mining	39
Following Labor Unrest	42

Community Leadership	45
A Wife and Family	48
Settling in Wilkes-Barre	50
Running for Office	54
Founding the Board of Trade	56
A Stint in the Pennsylvania House	66
Writing, Speaking, and Politics	74
A Move to Scranton	77

PART FOUR
Early Decline | 79

PART FIVE
Epilogue | 84

SIGNS OF THE TIMES | Scattered throughout

APPENDIX 1	C. Ben Johnson's Civil War Diary	89
APPENDIX 2	The Human Side of General George Washington	100
BIBLIOGRAPHY	103
LLUSTRATION SOURCES	106
INDEX	107

DEDICATION

For all the descendants of

C. BEN JOHNSON

...six generations and counting.

AUTHOR'S NOTE

During my first 50 years, my father had mentioned a couple times that a distant relative had been a drummer boy in the Civil War. When dad died some 25 years ago, his stash of family files and memorabilia, although thin, contained four artifacts hinting at a potentially interesting character. There were two letters to a C. Ben Johnson, one an 1871 note from Horace Greeley, and another from General William Tecumseh Sherman in 1888. And there was a small leather notebook with a few dozen newspaper clippings glued to the pages and commenting on a candidate for 'Reading Clerk' in the Pennsylvania House of Representatives in 1883. But the piece de resistance was a small, 56-page hand-written diary covering disparate periods between 1861 and 1863, during the Civil War.

Before and after those items moved from dad's drawer to my drawer in 1996, I heard, saw, and knew nothing more about this individual—my great, great grandfather Charles Benjamin Johnson.

In 2020, having finished off fun projects concerning two other ancestors, I decided to probe a bit into Johnson's life. I found some rich veins. Johnson lived at a time of extreme change and development on the North American continent, in the nascent United States, with the Civil War and the onset of the Industrial Revolution, and during a period of mass immigration. And in the thick of that changing world, C. Ben Johnson, as he was called, played a diverse and impactful role in and beyond his community of eastern Pennsylvania.

His story was little known and even less documented within our family, primarily because of patriarchy and politics. Ben and his wife had three daughters, one of whom married an Innes and had a daughter, who married a Turner and had twin boys, one of whom had me.

FROM CBJ TO THE AUTHOR

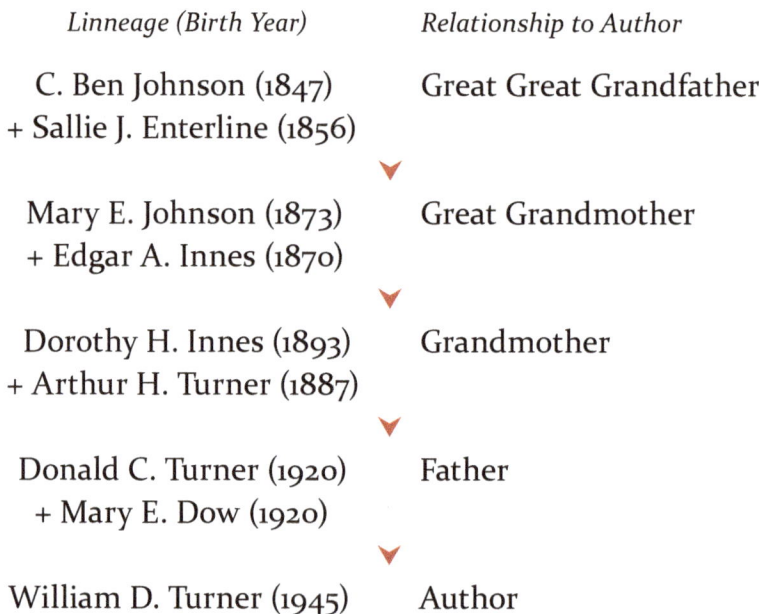

Linneage (Birth Year)	Relationship to Author
C. Ben Johnson (1847) + Sallie J. Enterline (1856)	Great Great Grandfather
Mary E. Johnson (1873) + Edgar A. Innes (1870)	Great Grandmother
Dorothy H. Innes (1893) + Arthur H. Turner (1887)	Grandmother
Donald C. Turner (1920) + Mary E. Dow (1920)	Father
William D. Turner (1945)	Author

During that 100-year period, education, careers, and most other important aspects of life were relegated and generally limited to males. (Recall that women could not even vote until 1920!) Ben Johnson was followed by two female generations and three generations of strong-willed male Turners. As a result, much family lore down through those generations was ignored or nipped in the bud, and little of C. Ben Johnson's story made it past his daughter, her daughter, and the Turners. And the first two generations of those Turners held to the strong English tradition of patriarchy with a misogynistic bent. As a result, the male line was traced and documented, the female line less so, barely at all.

There was also a political wind blowing against recognizing the life and activities of CBJ within the family, including among the Turner clan. As you will read, the common thread throughout Johnson's life after the Civil War was his views, work, writings, and causes in support of working people, satisfactory working conditions, civic duty, and workers' unions. The generations following CBJ—including the Turners, Inneses, Townends, Nesbits, and Butlers—all tended to be the landed, industrial, or military folks in the community, all wary of or hostile to unions and perhaps to populism in general. Thus, they would not be expected to highlight, commend, or document the worker and union causes that represented such an important part of CBJ's activities and contributions.

So, in a way we are lucky, and perhaps should be pleasantly surprised, that the novelty of a drummer boy relative—and my dad's holding onto those few artifacts—survived into the 21st Century and provided the strings to pull in tracing the life and times of C. Ben Johnson.

Note that everyone has 16 great, great grandparents, so chances are that some may be interesting.

WDT | Autumn, 2022

ACKNOWLEDGMENTS

AS ALREADY MENTIONED, the diary, notebook, two letters, and a few fleeting comments about a drummer boy from my father planted a small seed that took half a century to germinate.

With time on my hands, and my Aunt Sue's careful transcription of the diary to pour over, the internet—especially via Google, Ancestry and its Newspapers.com—became my primary researchers. Without these virtually boundless and efficient troves and search resources, the process of tracing C. Ben Johnson's activities and the things happening around him nearly two centuries ago would have far outlived me.

The Luzerne County Historical Society was helpful in identifying his movements around Wilkes-Barre, and a variety of sources listed in the Bibliography speak for themselves.

Special thanks go to my cousin Ellen Turner Scott—CBJ's great great granddaughter and keeper of her mother's and other family files—for digging up and providing five of the photos of Ben, Sallie and family that appear in the write-up.

And thanks to Curt Carpenter, who's editing, design, and publishing help make this volume possible.

Charles Benjamin Johnson | 1847–1907

PART ONE

Early Days, Hard Times, and the Call to War

A NASCENT USA

INTO THE THIRD CENTURY of gradual exploration and colonization of North America, Europeans had established the 13 colonies, which formed a country and government independent of English or other 'foreign' rule, settling and spreading generally from east to west across sparsely populated native-American lands.

With George Washington inaugurated only a decade before, the first half of the 19th century was a period of 'establishment' and the beginning of explosive growth across the continent. Indeed, the new nation grew from 16 states in 1800, to 31 states by 1850, and the population surged from five million to 23 million over those five decades.

The country's economic development became bifurcated by north and south, due to the climate for crops and tolerance of and dependence on slave labor in the South, and urban and industrial production in the North. Cotton, tobacco, and other crops became the mainstay of the expanding economy of the South. Industrialization and the onset of the industrial revolution, primarily in the North, emanated from the United Kingdom and Europe and fed on technological innovation, creating whole new industries based on transportation (canals, railroads, and later steam and internal combustion engines and airships), steel (along with coal mining and coke baking), and fossil fuels (extraction, refining, and heating).

Manufacturing—mills, factories, and steel production made possible by coal, and increased productivity made possible by new machines and factory workers—centered in the northeast, from Massachusetts down to Virginia. In the 'New England' and eastern seaboard regions, canals and rivers provided the primary commercial transportation and then gave way to the new and expanding networks of railroads. And waterpower became inflexible and insufficient and gave way to wood, coal, and eventually oil burning and electric sources of energy, power, and heat.

The westward 'manifest destiny' was boosted by the discovery of gold in California in 1848—just prior to C. Ben Johnson's second birthday. And the country was in a sense made whole, east to west, by completion of the transcontinental railroad in May of 1869.

This trajectory of growth and expansion would continue through the second half of the 1800s, with the U.S. population quadrupling again from 23 million in 1850 to 87 million in 1907, with 46 states by then, coast to coast.

PENNSYLVANIA

THE FIRST HALF OF THE 1800S had seen not only rapid development in the new nation's westerly geographic expansion, but also industrialization in the North that included Pennsylvania as a primary participant.

Originally a vast 1681 Royal Land Grant to William Penn, the state of Pennsylvania was at the center of this burgeoning industrial revolution, as it bordered both Lake Erie to the north and the Delaware River and Bay below Philadelphia at the southeast corner.

Pennsylvania grew as an economic engine, fueled by the rapid expansion of coal mining, railroads, petroleum, iron and steel production, and other manufacturing. With a population of 602,500 in 1800—second only to Virginia at that time—Pennsylvania grew to 2.3 million residents by 1850, exceeded then only by the State of New York with 3.1 million. And Pennsylvania's population would more than triple during the second half of the century, during Ben Johnson's life.

The area was never densely inhabited by Native Americans. No more than 20,000 Native Americans lived in all of Pennsylvania when white men first arrived from Europe, and by 1800, colonial expansion had forced most of them to leave. So, the 1871 Indian Appropriations Act had little effect in Eastern Pennsylvania, and there are no federally-recognized tribes in the state today. This is somewhat ironic, as so many places and natural features in the state acquired names derived from the pre-Revolutionary tribes and their languages.

And, although Philadelphia and other cities served as nodes on the 'underground railroad' for escaping slaves moving north during the Civil War, relatively few Blacks settled in the state during the decades after the War. Even today in Luzerne County, for example, African Americans account for about 5% of the population, less than half of the U.S.-wide make-up.

PHILADELPHIA

THE CITY OF PHILADELPHIA, having been the site of the drafting and passage of the Declaration of Independence and the Constitution, served as the nation's capital for the decade of the 1790s, while the District of Columbia was being built. The country's second largest city by population in 1800, with 41,000 residents, Philadelphia grew to 121,000 by 1850.

LINCOLN, WAR OF THE STATES, AND RAISING AN ARMY

SLAVERY HAD BECOME A DIVISIVE ISSUE in the new nation early on. The Missouri Compromise of 1820 saw the admission of both Maine and Missouri as new states, adding one where slavery was not allowed and the other without that prohibition. As the century unfolded, industrial growth in the north depended on immigrant workers—mostly from Europe and often subjected to subsistence pay and deplorable working conditions. But a fundamental driver of the north-south division was ownership and freedom of their respective workers.

Immediately after Abraham Lincoln's election as President in November 1860, the issue of slavery came to a boil with the secession of seven southern states by January of 1861, followed by establishment of the Confederate States of America, with its capital in Richmond and Jefferson Davis as its President. The spring and summer saw initial attacks and battles in South Carolina, Virginia, and Missouri, and Lincoln and the Union military went into recruiting mode as the Civil War geared up. In July and August, the Battle of Bull Run in Virginia and the Battle of Wilson's Creek in Missouri produced considerable Confederate advances in both the east and west and stirred the populations in the northern states to rapidly expand their military and volunteer forces.

Lincoln called on the governors of the Union states to organize and recruit more troops. Pennsylvania's Governor Andrew Curtin agreed to provide 25 regiments and ordered the formation of training camps across the state. This initiative eventually produced 270 Pennsylvania regiments and about 400,000 soldiers during the War, more than any other northern state except New York.

> **Signs of the Times**
>
> • In 1848, gold was discovered in California.
>
> • In 1859, conveniently extractable oil was discovered at Titusville, Pennsylvania, 100 miles north of Pittsburgh.

Curtin called on W.W.H. Davis, a 41-year-old prominent newspaper publisher in Doylestown—40 miles north of Philadelphia in Bucks County—to recruit a complement of troops from that area. Davis, who had served as an officer in the Mexican War, readily agreed on two conditions: First, that he would recruit only from Bucks County, and second, that all the troops raised would train locally—that is, at Doylestown, rather than at the state's capital of Harrisburg.

Davis received approval and authority for the arrangement in August 1861, and immediately began recruiting volunteers and organizing a training camp at the fairgrounds on the western edge of Doylestown. The training camp was named Camp Lacey, to commemorate a Revolutionary War General from Bucks County. On September 6, the first company was officially 'mustered' into service, and only eight weeks later, the regiment—the

Charles Benjamin Johnson
Drummer Boy, Company D 104 Pennsylvania Regiment

Fourteen years old | September, 1861

104th Pennsylvania Volunteer Infantry Regiment—contained 1,135 officers and men. Davis himself led the group as a Colonel and nicknamed it the 'Ringgold' regiment, after an officer who had served with him and was killed at the battle of Resaca de la Palma in Mexico. Locally, the regiment was also referred to as 'Bucks County's Own.'

ENTER C. BEN JOHNSON

CHARLES BENJAMIN JOHNSON'S LIFE began on January 15 in 1847 Philadelphia. Ben's father, John Marion Johnson, had moved from Baltimore to do business in Philadelphia, and Ben's mother, Mary Guilliam Johnson had immigrated to Philadelphia from Shrewsbury, England.

Ben attended public schools in Philadelphia and, evidently clever, was able to enter high school earlier than usual and before his age legally allowed. When his father's business fell on hard times, however, the financial strains caused Ben to drop out of school before graduating. By 1861, at age 14, he moved through a series of jobs, including making boys' shoe uppers, selling newspapers, and working in a few retail shops.

AN OFF RAMP AND AN ON RAMP

WHEN LINCOLN ISSUED his call for soldiers in 1861, 14-year-old Ben Johnson "was one of the first to respond," joining the Union war effort as a 'musician'—a drummer boy. He signed up and was mustered in at Quakertown on September 17, 1861, sworn in for a three-year stint in the Doylestown-based unit. Despite having resided in Philadelphia rather than in Bucks County, Ben was accepted, either under the cover of fibbing or more likely because they were determined to create as large a regiment as possible and looked the other way. He gave his age as 16 years. With other new recruits, he boarded at Orem's Hotel in Doylestown until the 104th Regiment of Pennsylvania Volunteers was officially established at Camp Lacey. By the end of September, Ben was ensconced in Company D of the 104th infantry unit, encamped in the Lacey tent city. Company D was under the command of Captain Jacob Swartzlander, and many of its Bucks County men were from Quakertown.

It is unclear exactly why Ben decided to join, but a combination of motivations probably contributed. It could well have been a case of running away from home. His personal and family situation was stressed financially and had forced him to take on menial jobs. Patriotism was running high in the Northeast and Eastern Seaboard, and the chance to serve the Union, see other parts of the country, and take on a paying job in the military probably was attractive to him. He was 14 and without training, skills, or plans about what to do with his life. As a result, enlisting provided an obvious exit from his current situation, while moving on with his life in the midst of the consuming event of the day—the War with the South.

A 'MUSICIAN' AT WAR

THE FEDERALLY MANDATED MINIMUM AGE for military service was 16, and Ben falsely said he met that requirement. Many of the younger boys either lied about their age or appeared old enough not to be asked for proof. And to avoid feeling guilty about lying, some wrote the number 18 on a piece of paper placed in their boot, in order to truthfully state they were "over 18" when asked. This was likely common among drummer boys, who were pervasive across Army units, but without combat roles. The youngest tended to end up as drummers, and the Army probably was keen to let the age requirement go unmet. Still, the average age of the drummers was 18, so Ben was very young, even among the musicians.

Some 3,900 boys served as drummers for the Union during the War, and the Confederate Army had at least that many as well, perhaps more. Drummers joined the soldiers in the battles, communicating tactical orders and conveying a wide variety of signals through their drumbeats. They were required to know dozens of drum 'calls,' and the playing of each call would tell the soldiers specific tasks they were required to perform.

A second role that became widespread for the drummer boys involved carrying stretchers and otherwise attending to and retrieving wounded and dead soldiers on the battlefields, both in real time during the battles and afterwards. As a result, although they were often stationed at the rear of squads while drumming, they were in harm's way, especially when in the line of fire and scrambling to recover the fallen. In some cases, drummers were quick to pick up firearms and use them either defensively to get away, or to carry on for fallen soldiers against the enemy.

Each unit usually had two drummers, and Ben's Company D filled the roles with Ben and Casper Somerdyke, who both joined the same day and were discharged the same day three years hence.

Some who signed up had played the drums as an instrument previously, and others learned just prior to enlisting. Many, though, including Ben, learned 'on the job.' There no doubt were 'wash outs,' as a reasonable level of skill was required, and the accuracy and effectiveness of drumbeats were crucial to manage the troops, win battles, and save lives.

It is interesting to note that three of Ben's important life events as a young boy were beyond or contrary to 'the rules' in an

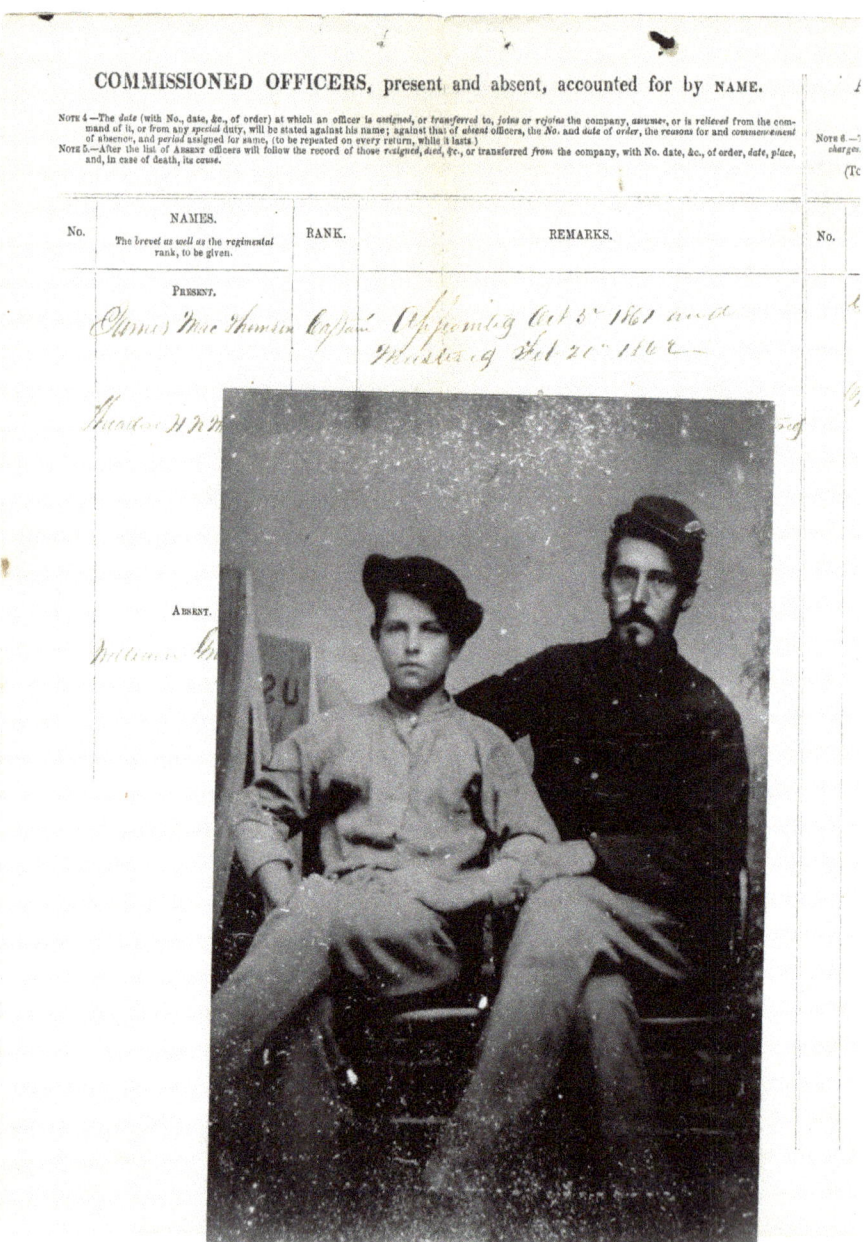

C. Ben Johnson and an unnamed officer | October 1861

American society that was still formalizing and not focused on strictly enforcing less important regulations. Ben had entered high school before reaching the required age, he had joined the Army before reaching the required age, and he had joined the Bucks County unit from Philadelphia.

BECOMING A SCRIBE

ALTHOUGH ONLY 14 when he joined up, C. Ben Johnson (the name form he preferred and by which he was mostly known all his life) kept a sporadic diary during the first year and a half of his stint—i.e., between August of 1861 and March 1863—as his outfit traveled from its Doylestown home base down the eastern seaboard. Although so young and not having completed high school, he was obviously bright and observant, and the writing is competent and descriptive, seemingly beyond his age. He felt a need and bothered to do it, he wrote clearly and well, and he kept what he wrote.

Ben was adept at conveying in writing where and when he was and what was happening to him and his outfit. However, the descriptions were light on his impressions, feelings, and interpretations about what was going on. And although drumming was his reason for being there—his job for four years, if you will—he says nothing in the diary about his drumming or its role in all the battles and travels in which he participated. In his pages of detailed write-ups, the word 'drum' appears only a single time, in mentioning that he and drummers from other companies shared a tent at one encampment.

The absence of interpretation and feelings imply a bit of distance, as a drummer boy, from the detailed day-to-day activities and involvement in the tactics and horrors of War—perhaps a result of his position as a musician without a musket.

C. Ben Johnson's original Civil War diary from 1861–1863 has been lost, but not before CBJ's great grandson's wife, Ellen Sue Turner, was able to photocopy and transcribe the pages.

He regularly refers to the soldiers as "the boys" in a fond way and without disparagement. Although constantly present and at risk on the march and at the battles, Ben's position seems to the reader more one of observer—somewhat akin to embedded journalists in later wars, but with little interpretation. Drummers were respected and supported by both his Union colleagues and the Confederate enemy, but perhaps they nevertheless felt a bit peripheral.

Even taking account of his young age and inexperience in life, the absence of analysis and interpretation is somewhat surprising when laid against his future career and writings that are full of strong causes, points of view, and personal opinions, are extensive and detailed, and filled Ben's robust public life.

The frequency and length of his diary writings declined over the months of 1862, ceasing altogether in the spring of 1863. If any additional write-ups were created, they have been lost.

Ben's writing interest and competence introduced in his early writing—by a 14-year-old high school drop-out—were to frame and be central to his later life and career in journalism, politics, and the advancement of the labor union movement in America.

PART TWO

Surviving Four Years of War

B EN'S DIARY gives us first-hand insight about where he was, what his unit was doing, and what was happening around them for the first two years of his involvement. Fortunately for us, the Civil War overall, the 104th Regiment, and the campaigns in which they participated are well documented. We can place his experiences and writings into the broader picture and, importantly, we can infer where he was and what he was doing in the last two years of his military service—that is, beyond the end of his diary.

From Ben's writings, we glean a few overarching conditions during his four years in the Union Army. Months at a time were spent merely getting from one place to another—almost always on foot ('marching'), sometimes by rail where and when there were rail lines, and occasionally by boat along the east coast, major bays, and major rivers. And transportation on foot made troop mobility exceedingly slow and time consuming, requiring weeks and months of amassing disparate troops into true armies that could then undertake the grand and decisive battles. Availability of rations—i.e., food—was a constant concern and constraint, with many routes, delays, and hardships determined by the search for vittles.

So, for Ben and the larger units of which his Company and the 104th became a part, the War consisted of marching, encamping, bivouacking, scrounging for food, strategizing and taking tactical actions involving setting pickets (i.e., lookouts), and moving from one usually rural location to another—each activity often consuming weeks or months at a time. As a result, although there were dozens of battles during the War, for many troops the actual battles were far from constant. Rather, they tended to be brief, wholly local, and intermittent, often with weeks or months in between.

And at those battles, artillery—when available and 'modern'—was crucial and helped determine their outcomes. Otherwise, the combat was entirely hand-to-hand and with rifle volleys.

THE ADVENTURES OF BEN AND THE 104TH

COMPANY D OF THE 104TH PENNSYLVANIA took part in three of the War's important theaters along the Eastern seaboard: the Peninsula Campaign in Virginia in 1862, including the battle of Fair Oaks-Seven Pines, where they received the brunt of a Confederate attack; the siege of Charleston, South Carolina and the attack on Fort Wagner during the winter of 1862/63; and the Shenandoah Valley Campaigns in 1864/65, including the Siege of Petersburg, Virginia.

As we follow Ben and the War through his unit's participation in the three major campaigns, all quotations contained in the following 10 pages are directly from his diary, unless otherwise noted. And all his comments—indicated by quotation marks and red text—contain the original spelling and punctuation as written. And, for reference, the entire typed diary—Memorandums of Chas. B. Johnson While Connected with Co. D 104 P.V.—is contained in Appendix 1.

The month of October 1861 was devoted to organizing, outfitting, and basic drills and marches. After the first march to a meeting, Ben commented,

"The place was about five miles and we thought it to be rather a hard march but we have since found out what hard marching is having had plenty of it to do." A few days later, the now-uniformed men *"drew their muskets and all seemed to be anxious to get where they could use them."* When they *"drew their caps, all thought they were soldiers now for a surety."*

The regiment attended a festive dinner in Hartzville, with speeches by Colonel Davis and Governor Curtin, among others.

"The regiment escorted the Governor to and from the [train] cars with the band playing and Colors flying."

On November 6, after six weeks of *"quiet and very easy times,"* the regiment took the 25-car train to Philadelphia and after a lunch and a march across town to the Baltimore Depot,

"we left Philadelphia amid the waving of handkerchiefs and the 'Good Byes' and 'God Bless Yous' of our friends."

The next day, they changed stations and trains in Baltimore and arrived in Washington in mid-afternoon.

"Here we had an apology for a meal in the shape of some coffee brought to us in horse buckets, salt beef and a dry crust."

They spent about six weeks encamped at Kalorama Heights near Georgetown—*"for amusement we had the Rock Creek for swimming."* Breakouts of smallpox and typhoid fever in the camp proved minor and short-lived, thanks to Colonel Davis's nearly obsessive sanitary enforcement.

Meanwhile, under the supervision of a Lieutenant Carver, a proper barracks was being built at nearby Meridian Hill, and the regiment moved into it on Christmas day 1861.

> *"The night of the 24th being Christmas Eve was passed very pleasantly, the boys having received a number of boxes of eatables from homes of which to make their Christmas Dinner."* The new bunks and comfort of Carver Barracks *"was as acceptable to us as a Christmas present as anything else could have been."*

The 104th regiment was part of the larger brigade—also headed by Colonel Davis—along with another Pennsylvania regiment, one from New York, and a fourth from Maine. They all spent the next three winter months in Washington

> *"...forever being reviewed or inspected"* and learning *"to drill and maneuver well under excellent and oft repeated tuition of our field officers."*

During the winter of 1861-62, the Colonel identified drinking as an immediate enemy. As Davis described in his memoirs:

> "Whisky was the most troublesome enemy the army had to fight during the winter. The proprietors of groggeries were almost legion in number and were found located on every side. Through the instrumentality of 'red eye' and 'tribulated tanglefoot,' many a good fellow was brought to grief."

Toward the end of March 1862, following the dull and muddy winter, the men were in high spirits to leave, and the brigade carried out formal drills

> *" for the first time and our brigade when drawn up in line of battle alone made a line three fourths of a mile long."*

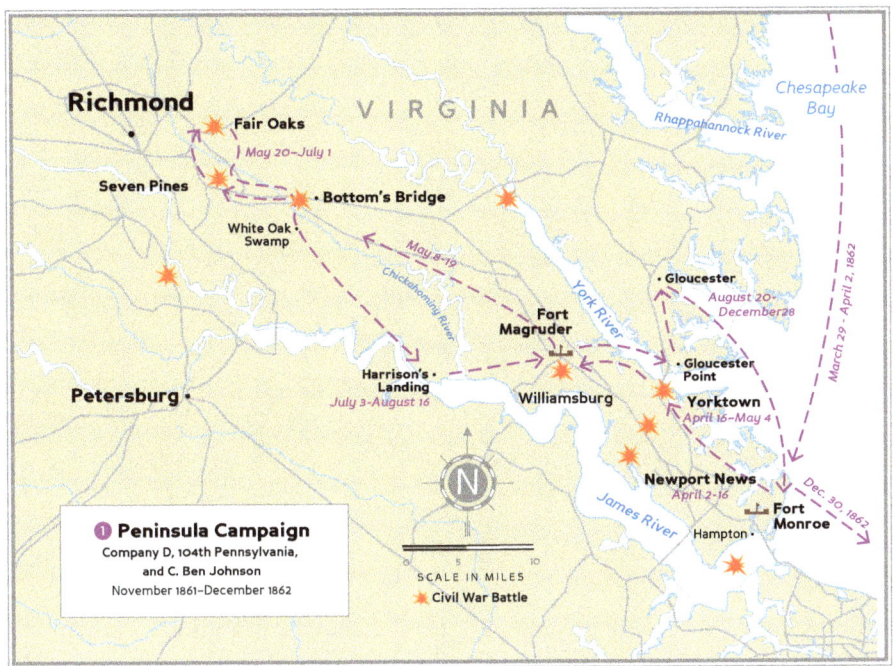

Peninsula Campaign | 1861-1862

They would not return to the Carver Barracks, because, upon their departure, the barracks were converted into the Carver General Hospital, one of Washington D.C.'s largest military hospitals.

THE PENINSULAR CAMPAIGN OF 1862

From March 29 to the 30th, they marched and camped on their way to the wharf at Alexandria, 10 miles down the Potomac from Meridian, suffering both marching and bivouacking in bitter cold, heavy snow and rain, and a lack of shelter. After spending a bad night on the docked *U.S.S. Constitution*, they transferred to the *State of Maine*, and at 11:00 AM on March 31 started down the river toward Fort Monroe, 200 miles south at the tip of the Virginia peninsula.

Hospital steamer *State of Maine* docked in Alexandria Virginia. With a capacity of 300 patients, the ship served primarily to bring wounded Union soldiers to medical facilities on the East Coast.

> "We had a good view of both shores and the interesting objects of each among which was Mount Vernon, the residence of Washington, and Fort Washington...we were saluted with three cheers from the troops there and a tune from their brass band."

They arrived at Fort Monroe on April 2 and spent the next two weeks—the beginning of the siege of Yorktown—camped in a peach orchard at Newport News and mostly drilling and picketing (i.e., manning armed lookout posts) in the surrounding swamps. On the 16th and 17th, they made their way 18 miles to Warwick Court House and then another few miles to just outside Yorktown.

> "On Easter Sunday the regiment was on Picket reserve in mud and water up to their knees."

These weeks saw the first firings at and from the enemy, as well as the first time the men were under enemy shelling. They lost two men, with another wounded. For the entire month of May,

> *"While we lay at this place which was called Camp Scott we had very poor rations."*

With the siege successfully complete on May 4, they marched away, first through the Rebel Forts at Yorktown, which were empty, then *"towards the James River, the Rebs evacuating as we advanced,"* and then towards Williamsburg, arriving a half mile from that battleground. May 5 saw the unit in the fit of battle all day and night, and they marched to and encamped at Fort Magruder the next day,

> *"tending to their wounded and burying their dead."*

From May 8 to 19th, they marched the 37 miles to the outskirts of Bottom's Bridge, encamping for the nights in a cornfield, the villages of Ropers Church and New Kent Center, and a sawmill along the R. & W. P. Railroad. Their first skirmish was at Bottom's Bridge on the 19th, as the regiment was caught between two artillery lines. They were ordered across the Chickahominy Creek on the 20th, and *"slept on our arms all that night,"* returning to camp for two day's rest.

On May 23 and 24, they marched on reconnaissance to Seven Pines and

> *"attacked the enemy's pickets"* in a *"brisk engagement."* An artillery battery *"soon moved up and in the course of two or three hours put the Rebs to a complete rout,"*

and they drove the enemy back about a mile. One Union soldier was killed, one severely wounded, one or two slightly wounded, and a Lieutenant Groff *"wounded in the breast by a six pound shot."*

By the 27th, they had moved a few miles onward to Fair Oaks, encamped...

"in front of a large woodpile," and, with a major battle brewing, on the 29th *"the boys were at work making an abattis of felled trees to prevent the Rebs from charging on our camp."*

On May 31, 1862, a captured Rebel Lieutenant told Ben's brass that an attack was set for that day, and

"Our regiment was immediately drawn up in line of battle...

"our pickets were soon seen coming out of the woods and whole columns of Rebs after them in hot pursuit. The fight soon began in earnest and in the course of three or four hours, no reinforcements coming up, our men were compelled to retreat hotly contesting every inch of the ground."

"The battle raged until dark when both armies stopped as if by mutual consent. We lost about half of the men we took into the fight in killed and wounded. Col. Davis was wounded in his right arm and breast. Maj. Gries was killed. Lieutenant McDowell of Co. K was killed and Capt. Swartzlander, Co D, Corcoran, Co. G, Orein, Co. B, Lieutenant Ashenfelder, Co. H, Lieutenant Kephardt, Co. B were wounded. This was one of the most bloody battles on record for the number of men engaged."

The next day, June 1,

"Fresh troops attacked the Rebs today and compelled them to retreat."

They made their way back to and across the Chickahominy Creek, wading through rain-fueled and sometimes waist-deep water, finally making camp on June 6 at a train station. Here they

"lay quietly" until June 28, when, with *"rumors of Jackson's Raid"* and hearing *"heavy firing on the right,"*

they recrossed the Creek and set up Rifle Pits and a line around Bottoms Bridge. With artillery assistance, they held that position for two days. They moved to the White Oak Swamp Bridge the evening of the 29th, and on the 30th were engaged in

"one of the heaviest artillery fights ever heard of"

all morning but suffered no casualties.

They marched on the morning of July 1, encountering the brunt of the Malvern Hill battle—as Ben described it:

"a scene which can be better imagined than described."

Union Howitzers at the Battle of Fair-Oaks/Seven Pines
May-June, 1862

The next day brought another skirmish at Carter's Hill, and on the 3rd, they marched the last seven miles to Harrison's Landing. Since leaving the Chickahominy on June 28, the regiment had been serving as Rear Guard of the wagon train, while also on Picket for a good portion of the journey.

Having established their camp at Harrison's Landing near the St. James River, General McClellan reviewed his entire army on July 4, and the 104th regiment remained there for more than a month to August 15. During that stay, with the men mostly picketing, they were also worked hard on Division Drill, with men often dropping from the summer heat. One or two died from heat stroke.

"It was whispered that" General Peck, who led the incessant drilling, *"had been indulging in something stronger than water."* Also, during these weeks, *"One night the Rebels opened forty pieces of artillery on us from the opposite side of the river, but our Gun Boats soon put a stop to them."*

On August 15, they built *"stuffed paddies"*—manikins or dummies—

"and posted them as sentinels on the ramparts of the rifle pits we had built while there. I can imagine the Rebs stealthily advancing on their harmless foes after we had evacuated that place."

And the next day, August 16, they all did leave camp and marched toward Williamsburg, to within six miles on the 17th—a total of about 25 miles. It was dusty and *"the rations very poor."* The following day, they passed through Williamsburg and camped just short of Yorktown, then spent the 19th foraging:

"beef, pork, fruit and in fact anything we could lay our

> *hands on. The beef tasted good although it was roasted or rather smoked on sticks and eaten without salt."*

At Yorktown on the 20th, they took the steamer *Mystic* to Gloucester Point on the opposite side of the York River, bivouacking outside the fort there, and moving into the fort the next day

> *"put up a very comfortable camp from the shelter tents we had with us and boards, of which there was a goodly quantity to be had."*

They were to remain there four months, until December 28, 1862.

On August 25th,

> *"the boys ransacked a Rebel Colonel's nearby house,"* taking *"chickens, ducks, geese, turkeys, watermelons and in fact everything in the eating line we could lay our hands on and in the evening returning nearly every man was stocked with eatables enough for a while at least."*

On November 16, there were reports that Confederates were advancing on the picket line, and Company D was sent out as a Picket Reserve. An enemy squadron of about 60 cavalrymen appeared and

> *"poured in a volley from their carbines and pistols,"*

killing one, wounding two, and taking away three prisoners.

The rest of the stay was

> *"a pretty as well as comfortable camp." "The drummers tented together while here and we had pleasant times."*

THE SIEGE OF CHARLESTON | 1863-64

ON DECEMBER 28, 1862, they embarked on the sailing vessel *Wm. Woodbarry* and were towed on the 29th to Fort Monroe by the tug *Jas. J. Treeborne*, continuing past Cape Henry on the 30th, and anchoring off the bar at Beaufort Isle on January 2, due to persistent storms. They disembarked the next day at Morehead City, North Carolina, and marched to and encamped at Carolina City on the banks of Boque Sound. In a rare bit of sarcasm, Ben describes:

> *"The city is beautiful large place and consists of the Justice's and Shoemaker's house both in one, a rail road depot, a barn, stable and pig pen."* It *"was rainy and windy and very cold...very disagreeable."*

The stay at Carolina City was 18 days. On January 21, 1863, they boarded the vessel *Cahawba* at the Morehead City wharf but did not get away from the harbor until the 25th, after grounding on a sand bar and then colliding with a steamer. And it took a further two weeks—until February 10th—to reach and get *"fairly landed on St. Helena Island,"* South Carolina, the delay due primarily to continued stormy weather.

Although Ben's notes end at this point during the War, the record of his and his unit's further endeavors is well documented. And Ben continued in the musician role for the rest of the War.

The unit—that is, Company D of the 104th Regiment, which was attached to a sequence of brigades over the course of the War—spent the next 18 months positioning, planning, and taking various actions against the Confederate port city of Charleston and its key Forts Sumter and Wagner.

Moving among the islands approaching the harbor—including the islands of St. Helena, Edisto, Morris, Folly, James, and

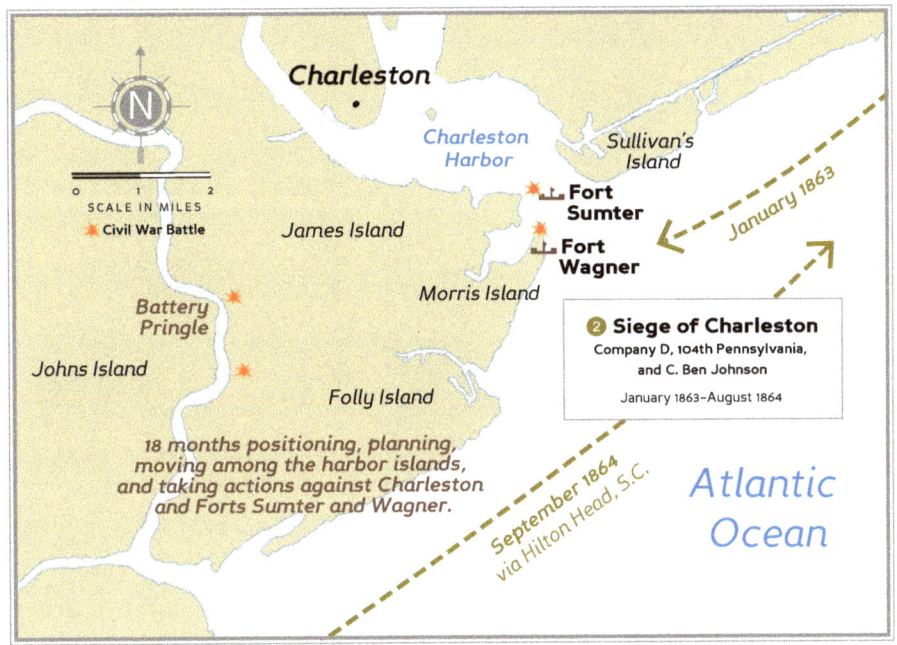

Siege of Charleston, South Carolina | 1863–1864

John's—they conducted expeditions against Charleston, James Island, and John's Island over these months.

On July 18, 1863, they mounted an attack on Fort Wagner. With high casualty rates from previous attempts in mind, the 3,000 troops were conscious that many would likely die and, after writing letters to those at home and leaving valuables with buddies, they steeled themselves mentally. But when they approached and entered the fort, they found it had been completely abandoned, marking a Union takeover of the Fort and possession of the entirety of Morris Island.

During their long siege on Morris, the bread provided by the Union army was considered inedible. So, Colonel Davis obtained some small bake ovens to allow the soldiers to bake their own. They were charged a nickel for each loaf, with the accumulating funds to be distributed among the soldiers at the War's end.

Steamship *Cahawba* sailed out of Mobile, Alabama between New Orleans, Havana, and New York. Later she joined the Confederate Navy.

For nearly the next year, the 104th was a defender of Fort Wagner and Morris and also carried out sporadic operations against Fort Sumter, Charleston, Battery Pringle, and others. In April 1864, while camped on Morris Island,

> *"The high tides were rising steadily from when the regiment first landed on the island the previous summer, but the men moved their tents upshore to weather the winter. Using scavenged pieces of boards and parts of cracker boxes, many were able to raise their tents above the sand or dig wind-protected 'basements' below."*

An unsuccessful attempt to capture the city of Charleston in early July 1864 brought to an end that long posting, and the regiment returned to its former camp at Hilton Head Island.

Colonel Davis was awarded a brevetted rank of Brigadier General

> *"for gallant and meritorious services during operations against Charleston."*

Within a month, they were sent to Florida to guard a railroad line, but after only a few weeks, went back north all the way to

Alexandria, to help defend the forts south of the Potomac until their enlistments expired in September.

The regiment—with Ben included—left Washington September 23, arriving in Philadelphia on the 25th. The Federal authorities gave a formal reception on the 27th, and, after staying a few days at the Volunteer Refreshment Saloon, they were all mustered out of service upon the expiration of their term on September 30, 1864.

Ben and many others immediately joined up again—in the Seventh (regiment) United States Veteran Volunteers—for what became the final year of the War, being finally discharged less than a year later. He spent this final stint with his former unit, as if his status had never changed, although he was now categorized as a Private.

THE SHENANDOAH VALLEY CAMPAIGN | 1864-65

THE UNIT WAS ORDERED TO HARPER'S FERRY, West Virginia, to escort a train of 600 wagons to Sheridan's army at Harrisburg, and then another train to Martinsburg. Moving to Philadelphia until after President Lincoln's reelection on November 4, 1864, they then joined the Army of the Potomac at Bermuda Hundred, Virginia, in late November. They remained on the center of the line between Appomattox and the James River all winter, until the fall of Petersburg ("Grant's utter failure") and Richmond on April 2, 1865, and Lee's surrender at Appomattox Court House a week later. They then occupied Petersburg for the next six weeks. By May 24, they had moved down to Fort Monroe and Norfolk, and were mustered out across the river in Portsmouth on August 25.

It seems, however, that earlier—in mid-February—Ben Johnson was 'paroled' from the unit and joined some other Pennsylvania

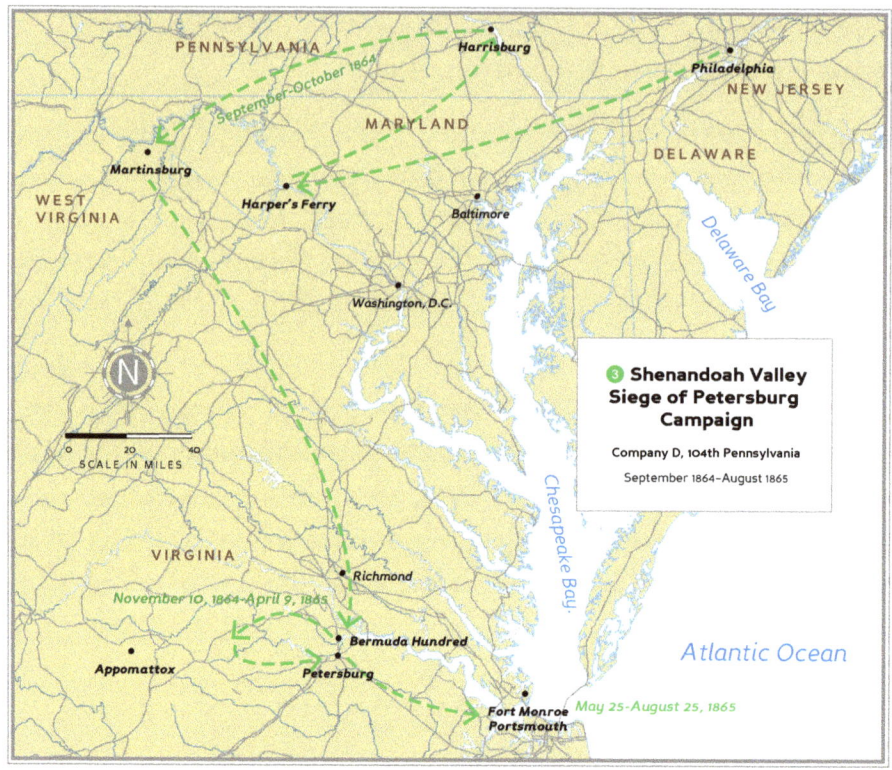

Shenandoah Valley Campaign | 1864–1865

and Maryland volunteers to exchange Union prisoners on a boat from Richmond. Via Aiken's Landing, then down the James River and up Chesapeake Bay, he arrived at Annapolis on February 27, 1865. He mustered out there, some six months earlier than the entire Seventh Regiment, and made his way back to Philadelphia and Bucks County.

Ben and his colleague drummer Casper Somerdyke had survived, and total regimental losses were modest by Civil War measures. The 104th lost two officers and 68 enlisted men killed or mortally wounded. Another 115 enlisted men died from diseases during the four years of fighting, two-thirds more than were lost in combat.

Shenandoah Valley Campaign | 1864–1865

MEMORIAL DAY AND GRAND ARMY OF THE REPUBLIC

BEFORE LEAVING WASHINGTON in the fall of 1864, and with the consent of the Secretary of War, the enlisted men of the 104th had voted to use their accumulated bread fund to erect in Doylestown a monument to the memory of their comrades who had fallen. At the War's end, the total collected was $1,600, augmented by private citizens—Colonel Davis and several others—to total a bit more than $3,000. This paid for the 34-foot high, white marble obelisk memorial, which was designed and built over two years. Erected in the center of town in 1867, the formal dedication took place on May 30, 1868.

The ceremony in the Doylestown town square was followed by the townspeople walking from the town center to the old fairgrounds that served as Camp Lacey, a distance of about a half mile. This 'parade' stands as one of the very first Memorial Day parades and makes the annual Doylestown event one of the country's longest continuous celebrations. In fact, the focus

This lithographed, 16" x 20" 'poster' was produced after the war, displaying the names by rank of all members of Company D of the 104th. One of the rare prints was part of an impressive collection of Civil War items owned by Captain Jacob Swartzlander, Company D's commanding officer. The roster includes, at the center bottom of the illustrated document:

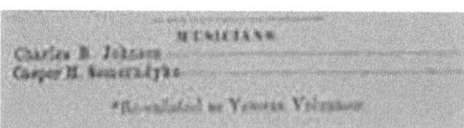

on dedication of the marble memorial itself may have given the holiday its ongoing name, which was originally 'Decoration Day' designed to decorate soldiers' graves.

* * *

IN APRIL OF 1866, the year following the War's end, Dr. Benjamin F. Stephenson, a Union Army veteran in Decatur, Illinois, founded a fraternal organization of military veterans of the War, comprising men who served between 1861 and 1866 in the Army, Navy, Marines, and 'Revenue Cutter Service' (precursor of the Coast Guard). Named the Grand Army of the Republic—G.A.R.—the first local 'post' in Decatur was soon replicated across the country, mostly in the North but also a few in the South and West. (The United Confederate Veterans was a similar organization for veterans in the South.)

On May 5, 1868, through General Order No. 11, G.A.R.'s first national Commander-in-Chief, General John A. Logan from Illinois, declared May 30 to be Decoration Day, calling on the membership to make the observance an annual event, which indeed has survived as a national observance and holiday.

Open only to Civil War veterans, the G.A.R. grew to peek membership at 490,000 in 1890 and survived for nearly 90 years. It dissolved in 1956 at the death of its last member, Albert Woolson of Duluth, Minnesota, aged 106.

Linking men through their experience of the war, the G.A.R. became among the first organized advocacy groups in American politics, supporting voting rights for black veterans, promoting patriotic education, helping to make Memorial Day a national holiday, lobbying the United States Congress to establish regular veterans' pensions, and supporting mostly Republican political candidates.

104th Pennsylvania Regiment
Memorial
Main and Court Streets
Doylestown, Bucks County, Pa.

**Erected 1867
Dedicated May 30, 1868**

**TO THE MEMORY OF
THE OFFICERS AND MEN
OF THE
ONE HUNDRED AND FOURTH
PENNSYLVANIA REGIMENT
WHO FELL IN THE LATE WAR**

Their good swords rust,
And their steeds are dust,
But their souls are with the saints
we trust.

The G.A.R. Medal

Originally formed to provide veterans local networks to maintain connections with each other and preserve camaraderie and 'fellowship,' the membership—hundreds of posts linked together as statewide 'departments' and further linked together nationally—became the de facto political arm of the Republican Party and was active and influential throughout the decades of Reconstruction. Five Presidents were G.A.R. members—Grant, Hayes, Garfield, Harrison, and McKinley.

Besides often wearing military-style uniforms, hundreds and thousands of members gathered for annual national conventions, with many wearing the official G.A.R. 'medal.'

Similar or parallel organizations—also using the local post/department/national structure—sprung up following wars into the 20th Century, most notably the Veterans of Foreign Wars and the American Legion.

* * *

C. BEN JOHNSON'S participation in the G.A.R. was extensive. Despite the organization's general alignment and political involvement with the Republican Party, and Ben's firm embrace of popular, progressive, and Democratic Party politics, their interests and causes overlapped significantly. With his lifelong causes of opportunity, working conditions, treatment of immigrants, and unions—and with a firm anti-slavery posture—Ben was no doubt sympathetic and a strong advocate

PART TWO | 35

for post-War black rights and equal treatment.

He very likely was present at and supportive of the Civil War monument dedication ceremonies in 1868 at Doylestown, when he was 21 years old and living close by. Twenty years later, Ben's correspondence with General W.T. Sherman in 1888 concerned in part the upcoming G.A.R. National Encampment to be held in September of that year in Cleveland, Ohio. And in 1890, Ben was commander of the Conyngham G.A.R. Post 97 in Wilkes-Barre and oversaw construction of the formidable Memorial Hall on South Main Street.

In promoting voting rights for Negro veterans—as many white veterans recognized their demonstrated patriotism and sacrifices—the G.A.R. became "one of the first racially integrated social/fraternal organizations in America. Black veterans, who enthusiastically embraced the message of equality, shunned black veterans' organizations in preference for racially inclusive and integrated groups. But when the Republican Party's commitment to reform in the South gradually decreased, the G.A.R.'s mission became ill-defined and the organization floundered," with many departments and posts disappearing in the 1870s.

New leadership revived the organization in the 1880s, advocating strongly for Federal pensions for veterans, and with black veterans joining in significant numbers and organizing new local posts. But without pressing the case nationally with Congress, pensions or remuneration for wounds to black soldiers never materialized.

Conyngham G.A.R. Post No. 97's Memorial Hall, 146 South Main Street, Wilkes-Barre, c. 1965. The Post was disbanded and the building sold in 1941 and demolished in the late 1960s.

PART THREE
Pursuing Journalism and Many Causes

A FTER LEAVING THE ARMY early in 1865, Ben Johnson returned to Pennsylvania and looked to find gainful employment and pursue his writing and 'reporting.' He eschewed the big city of Philadelphia and found his way to Doylestown and the nearby Bucks and Schuylkill County towns. By 1868, he was working in Tamaqua as a reporter/writer at a budding labor union publication—the *Anthracite Monitor*—aside the publication's founding editor and original owner William H. Sylvis. Ben never again would live in Philadelphia, unlike his parents, brother, and two sisters, who remained there throughout their lives.

WRITING ABOUT COAL AND WORKERS

THE MONITOR was the principal publication of the Workingman's Benefit Association (WBA), a new and influential local branch of the nascent National Labor Union. Ben's work there not only gave him his first position of influence using the power of words and letters, but also initiated his lifelong interest and involvement in advancing the interests of working people and in improving the coal-area communities around him.

THE RISE OF ANTHRACITE MINING

IT WAS A TIME OF GROWTH, growing pains, and the advent of many new institutions in central Pennsylvania. Anthracite coal and its mining became highly desirable and replaced bituminous (soft) coal as the ideal source of heat for the new and burgeoning steel mills in both nearby Bucks county and in the western part of the state around Pittsburgh.

Although Anthracite—or 'hard coal'—had been used as early as the 18th Century in some industrial furnaces, it was considered unburnable or too difficult to ignite, and virtually all Americans heated their homes and cooked with wood-burning stoves. In 1808, however, Jesse Fell, a Wilkes-Barre nail maker, tavern owner, and at that time the town's burgess, or mayor, "became convinced that anthracite could be kept at a continuous state of combustion by utilizing an open grate that allowed a minimum draft or steady flow of air." His fabricated grid worked well in the tavern and sparked a transformation in domestic cooking and heating across the country and furthering coal as the primary industrial energy source. As the commemorative plaque at the site of the tavern states, "This famed experiment spurted the rise of the anthracite industry & the Wyoming Valley's growth."

Lying mostly within Luzerne County in northeastern Pennsylvania, the Wyoming Valley is an oval-shaped area 16 miles long and three miles wide, bisected by the winding Susquehanna River. Its name derives from a Lenape Native American word meaning 'at the big river flat.' The name was in general use before the Revolutionary War Battle of Wyoming in 1778. (By the 1860's, most of the Lenape people of New Jersey, Pennsylvania, and New York had been 'removed' to the Oklahoma area.)

As the driving economic force in the area, there were four pri-

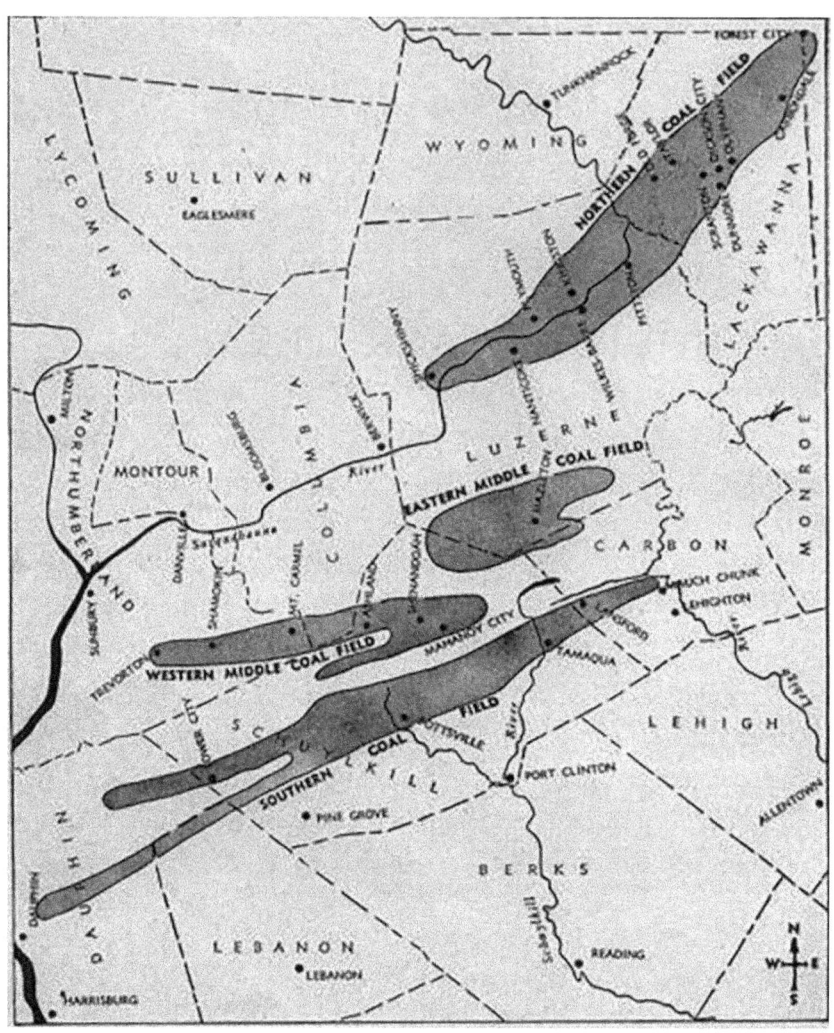

A map of the four anthracite coal fields of Pennsylvania

mary Anthracite coal fields—named the Northern, Eastern Middle, Western Middle, and Southern—running northeast to southwest and concentrated principally in Luzerne and Schuylkill counties.

Transportation of coal and steel—and people and other goods—drove the development and use of railroads, supplanting the dependence on horse-drawn rigs and river and canal boats. With extensive new railroad networks serving the Wilkes-Barre area, many other industries established mills, plants, and commercial businesses throughout the adjoining counties.

The steel plants and many other factories, the railroads, and especially the mining companies required thousands of unskilled workers, attracting waves of immigrants, mostly European laborers hoping to better their lots in America. The employers held the upper hand in paying and deploying these workers, resulting in many instances of unhealthy working conditions, low or subsistence pay, and sometimes untoward work for children. Exploitation of workers spawned the need for minimum working conditions and other reforms and protections and led to the call for 'collective bargaining' among and across worker groups and the formalization of labor unions.

Beginning in the early 1860s, some Irish workers used violence to advance their cause by killing mine owners, superintendents, bosses, and workers. Although never proven, this rash of violence has been ascribed to the Molly Maguires, a secret society named for a generally peaceful fraternal organization in Ireland, called the Ancient Order of Hibernians (AOH). Triggered by resistance to the Union Army draft and in support of organizing against mine owners, a wave of eight assassinations began in 1862 with the killing of mine foreman Frank W. Langdon. (This was not adjudicated until the 1878, however, with the

AOH leader, John Kehoe, hanged for the Langdon murder that had occurred 16 years earlier.)

FOLLOWING LABOR UNREST

IN AUGUST OF 1869, the Congress of the National Labor Union convened in Philadelphia and announced a number of committees to take their case forward. On the third day of the convention, *Monitor* writer Ben Johnson was appointed to the Committee of Labor Organ.

In 1871, Ben became the Editor of the *Anthracite Monitor* at age 24. From the beginning, he was a forceful proponent of the mission and activities of the Workingmen's Benevolent Association (WBA), the welfare of its union members, and nonviolence in all its activities. From his positions at several area newspapers over the next decade, Ben covered most of the early labor scene, providing him a platform for actively participating in and influencing a wide variety of community organizations and activities.

In the fall of his first year as Editor of the *Monitor*, Ben created a newsletter entitled the *Labor Reformer* that elicited a sharp response from the more employer-oriented *Wilkes-Barre Union* newspaper. Critiquing Ben's new paper, the *Union* editorial stated, "the object of the enterprise seems to be to instruct the workingmen of the State how they can most effectively perpetrate social and political suicide," and "we do not see that the paper in question has any particular mission, except to play into the interest of the Radical party." It concludes, "The sheet is diminutive in size, and we trust that its influence will be commensurate with its dimensions."

* * *

BETWEEN 1862 AND 1871, nobody had been convicted of eight Molly Maguire killings. But the *Monitor* was sure that the Molly Maguires were responsible and condemned the assassins in no uncertain terms. On December 9, 1871, the newspaper reported that Morgan Powell had been "murdered in cold blood at Summit Hill, by one of three dastards, who, with a pistol held close to his breast, fired the shot. Mr. Powell is said to have been especially well thought of by the men in the employ of the coal company; and among the community in which he lived, had many warm friends."

A second wave of Molly Maguire violence took place in 1875, when the first 'united' union comprising Irish, British, and American workers of all skill levels—the Workingmen's Benevolent Association—collapsed. Filling the anti-employer vacuum, the Molly Maguires reportedly carried out six assassinations that summer, with 10 others later also attributed to them.

Franklin B. Gowen, head of the Philadelphia & Reading Railroad led the pursuit of the Molly Maguires. He hired Allan Pinkerton as a private detective, to establish a company police force and hold the Mollys to account. Pinkerton in turn hired an Irish-born agent, James McParlan to infiltrate the company. Based on that work and the evidence produced, 10 men were charged, convicted and hanged in Pottsville and Mauch Chunk (a town name later changed to Jim Thorpe) on June 21, 1877, which became known to the people of the region as 'Black Thursday' or 'the day of the rope.' Ten more were hanged over the next three years, including John Kehoe for the Langdon murder.

* * *

AMONG THE VARIOUS FACTIONS and institutions that made up the social structure of the anthracite region, the WBA "vied with the Catholic church as the most unequivocal opponent of violence." During the 1860s and 1870s, the employers and even state government authorities had frequent episodes of violence, as did the Molly Maguires, supposedly on the workers' behalf. But trade union leaders "sought to bargain with their enemies rather than threaten, attack, or kill them. Explicit condemnation of the violent strategy of the Molly Maguires was part of the official policy of the WBA from the beginning" and its leader, John Siney, insisted that violence was strictly forbidden, "under pain of expulsion."

In his first editorial job at the *Monitor*, and then as its editor from 1871, Ben Johnson was a forceful proponent of the mission and activities of the WBA, the welfare of its union members, and nonviolence in all its activities.

In positions of journalistic influence, and with a knowledge of and advocacy for better working conditions and worker wellbeing, Ben had quickly come to be an objective and respected voice for the unions and their members' interests, but with a strong anti-violence position and without an anti-industry or revolutionary taint. A prolific writer and expresser of progressive opinions, he gained a positive reputation on all sides. And from his days

> **Signs of the Times**
>
> • In 1870, the 15th Amendment grants suffrage to African American men.
>
> • In 1871, the Indian Appropriations Act makes Native Americans legally wards of the nation.
>
> • The Financial Panic of 1873 begins a five-year economic depression.
>
> • 1873 ends an eight-year period of recurring epidemics, during which smallpox, cholera, typhus, typhoid, scarlet fever, and yellow fever killed thousands.

at *Monitor* onward, his point of view and causes fortified the missions of his organizations and constituencies, not vice versa.

COMMUNITY LEADERSHIP

IN 1871, about the time he became Editor, Ben was one of the ten charter members of a new Masonic lodge in his town of Tamaqua—the Tamaqua Circle, No. 52, Brotherhood of the Union.

On December 3, 1871, Ben received a letter from the nationally known founder and publisher of the *New York Tribune*, Horace Greeley. Greeley was one of the five founders of the Republican Party in 1854, a vigorous abolitionist throughout the 1850s, and was about to run for President as a Liberal Republican in 1872. Despite having Democrat endorsements, he lost in a landslide and died just weeks after the election. He also is remembered for his advice "Go West young man and grow up with the country." Although this well-known comment implies a way to advance the western migration or Manifest Destiny, it was prompted as a suggestion aimed at avoiding problems of poverty and unemployment characteristic of the big Eastern cities at the time. (As a result of Greeley's high-profile emphasis on western movement, a Colorado town was named in his honor in 1875.)

Greeley's letter was in response to an inquiry Ben had made concerning worker hours and pay, and the widely-held union proposition for imposing an 'eight hour day' rule, which acquired the label Eight Hour Movement. (Greeley's note was forwarded to our family decades later in an envelope from C.M. Sitgreaves, General Agent, Wyoming Valley Sanitarium, Room 9, Laning Building, Wilkes-Barre. Ben was Secretary and General Manager of the Sanitarium in the 1890s.)

Letter to C. Ben Johnson from publisher and Republican Party co-founder
Horace Greeley | December 3, 1871

THE LETTER:

Dec. 3, 1871

My Dear Sir:

I have yours of the 20th October this moment, having been off in New York since on Thanksgiving.

I do not think I could agree to the Reformers' sweeping proposition that Hired Labor is not well paid. My experience in every xxx of labor convinces me that those who sell their labor for money are as fairly recompensed as those who employ and pay themselves.

As to the Eight Hour rule, I have never yet been able to reduce my own hours of labor to eight per day; but that is no rule for others. I would like much to see 'a positive xxx xxxx of the days' work of all persons under 18 years of age to expect per day. I often find that the vigor of youth is often sapped by excessive hours of toil.

I took much interest at the outset in the Eight-Hour Movement, hoping? xxx good xxx… However, I thought I saw that where labor is audacious, and able to be xxxx by cold, rain, etc. it would? not be xxx to restrict it to 8 hours of good weather and no work at all at other times. But it seems to me that most xxx-xxx men simply want to be paid a ten-hour price doing eight hours work. I do not consider this fair nor even practicable. But if workmen would say "Reduce our hours to 8 per day and pay us in "satisfaction," I xxx xx back them right xxx.

My friend, I can sense? you to be a diligent worker. I am of that sort. We must not try to make this world a paradise for shirkers and xxx, for God will not consent to that. But if you will show me how to make Labor more effective, I

PART THREE | 47

think I can? see xxx to secure its better xxx.

*Yours,
Horace Greeley*
C. BEN JOHNSON, ESQ.

Horace Greeley stamp was first issued in 1961

Although Greeley and his publication were generally pro-labor for all the right reasons, he seems skeptical of the 'affordability' of paying the same wages for fewer or limited hours. He expresses this to Ben by suggesting workers should be willing to accept greater "satisfaction" instead of higher pay, and especially fears more pay for less work time without greater productivity.

A WIFE AND FAMILY

ON MAY 17, 1872, 25-year-old Ben Johnson married fifteen-year-old Sallie J. Enterline (born June 4, 1856), a member of the local Enterline family in Tamaqua. Her deceased father, Edward Enterline was a prosperous farmer and a 'leading citizen' of Tamaqua. An ancestor, Lutheran minister Michael Enterline, had come to the English colonies from Germany or Holland in 1765 to establish the Lutheran church in America. (Ben, however, remained a declared Universalist, and it is unclear what role religion played in his thoughts and life. And Sallie remained a practicing member of St. Stephen's Episcopal Church in Wilkes-Barre for the last 68 years of her life.) The wedding was at Pottsville, Schuykill County.

Ben's high profile and reputation and as a journalist, and the respect garnered, brought with it some tongue-in-cheek press coverage of his wedding, including an article in the *Machinists*

Sallie Enterline Johnson some years after her 1872 wedding to C. Ben Johnson.

and Blacksmiths International Journal a few months following the wedding:

A BOLD ROBBERY

The heretofore highly esteemed and much-respected editor of The Antracite Monitor, *C. Ben Johnson, has got himself into difficulty at last. He has for some time past been seen prowling around the premises of Edward Enterline, Esq., of Tamaqua, Pennsylvania. Although things looked rather suspicious, and Mr. Enterline had a hint of the intentions of this man, yet no one would venture an opinion until recently, when the property of Mr. Enterline was seized and carried to Pottsville, where a clerical gentleman gave Mr. Johnson a life-long dispensation to appropriate the theft to his own use. The whole affair is simply outrageous.*

Sallie and Ben subsequently had three daughters, the first being Mary Eva Johnson (born March 14, 1873) who married Edgar Innes and had a daughter, Dorothy Howard Innes (born May 7, 1893), this author's paternal grandmother.

Second daughter Gertrude Craige Johnson (born March 2, 1875) died at age nine in 1884. And a third baby girl, Florence, died soon after her birth in 1878. As a result, Mary remained their only child after 1884.

SETTLING IN WILKES-BARRE

THE MONITOR went bankrupt in 1873 for lack of funding, but was succeeded by the debt-ridden and sporadically published *Pottsville Workingman* (a four-page weekly), along with *The Labor Reformer,* both official organs of the Miners' Association of the Anthracite Counties. At first, owner John Siney named Robert Morgan as editor of the *Workingman,* but CBJ became Editor in June 1874. Former boss and owner Siney had moved to Cleveland as head of the recently formed Miners' National Union.

The WBA itself collapsed in 1875, and in that same year, Ben became Secretary of the Miners' Association in Pottsville. And after a decade at the *Monitor* and its replacements, Ben, Sallie, and their two young girls moved 38 miles north from Tamaqua to Wilkes-Barre in Luzerne County, as Ben joined the editing staff of the *Wilkes-Barre Sunday Leader,* then a widely circulated weekly newspaper. He was to remain at the Leader for the next eight years.

Ben brought the *Workingman* publication with him from Pottsville to Wilkes-Barre for at least a year, and it was met with some respect locally: "It represents the workingmen's interests and is independent of party. Such a journal should be supported generously by the laboring masses."

In this period, and reflective of Ben's notoriety as a top journalist, several publications in other cities tried to recruit him for top posts. For example, in early 1878, he was offered the editorship of both the "first-class daily paper in Altoona," and the *Industrial Advocate* in Scranton. Press coverage of the offers opined, "Wherever Mr. Johnson may be, he will assuredly give universal satisfaction to his readers."

He declined to take up these offers, but in May of 1878, joined the State of Pennsylvania's Auditor General's department in Harrisburg for a four-month stint at the request of that department's new manager. Returning to Wilkes-Barre to take up an editorial position on the *Leader* in October, the press noted, "Journalism is more congenial to him than the clerkship he now holds, hence the change."

Later that month, the Democratic County Committee hosted a large meeting in the township of Plains, two miles north of Wilkes-Barre. With music provided by the Silver Cornet Band, Ben was introduced as the first speaker and delivered a technical and sophisticated discussion of financial policy.

> *The Democratic doctrine,* he said, *was the doctrine of gold, silver and just as much legal tender currency as the government can float without its depreciating below the par of gold. Such a currency would tend to a more equitable distribution of the products of labor between labor and capital, and would not involve any of the dangers of National bankism....*

Beyond demonstrating the breadth of Ben's interests and expertise, this important but potentially dry subject was brought to life by his evidently nearl-magic public speaking ability. A

Downtown Wilkes-Barre | c.1870

review of the talk indicated: "The speaker interspersed his argument with a number of witty and appropriate stories, and held his audience, without losing a man, for a full hour and a half."

IN 1879, four years after Ben joined the *Wilkes-Barre Sunday Leader*, he and publisher Joseph Bogert launched a new afternoon paper. The *Pottsville Chronicle* called it "a live spicy daily." Its announcement:

> The Daily Union Leader *is the title of a new afternoon paper launched on the sea of journalism at Wilkes-Barre, by Joseph K. Bogert. The initial number...bears the appearance of a live, spicy daily, and just such a publication as the people*

of Luzerne County will appreciate. The field of afternoon journalism in Luzerne was left bare when the Record of the Times *changed to a morning publication, and the* Union-Leader *has now stepped in and occupied the ground. C. Ben Johnson will have editorial charge of the new venture and its columns will teem with bright and racy articles. Success to it.*

* * *

IN MARCH OF 1881, a Mrs. Seeley, who lived in the town of Tunkhannock—about 25 miles north of Wilkes-Barre—had sued the *News Dealer* for libel as a result of a reference to her published in the paper. On an unrelated trip to Tunkhannock, Ben Johnson encountered "friends of Mrs. Seeley" and was "roughly handled" in an ensuing quarrel. "Subsequently, he was arrested on a charge of assault and battery and locked up." However, he was soon released and went home. The next day, *the Wilkes-Barre Times* noted that "His face bears marks of hard usage."

> **Signs of the Times**
>
> • The name of the city of Wilkes-Barre combined two 18th Century English politicians—John Wilkes and Isaac Barre—who never left England or set foot in America but strongly supported the American Colonies and opposed many of the restrictive and exploitive British policies toward the Colonies in the 1780s. They were "zealous advocates of the American cause." The locals on the Susquehanna River adopted Wilkes Barre for their city's name, with the hyphenation coming into general use only after the 1840s. In reference to the shape of the town's Public Square, and as the value of the Anthracite coal became clear near the end of the 19th Century, folks began referring to Wilkes-Barre as the 'Diamond City.'

* * *

PART THREE | 53

IN 1883, Ben Johnson was made Secretary of the Democratic County Convention Committee for Luzerne County, a position he held for several years. In that role, he authored the rules governing the party, "under which the unseemly quarrels and disorder that used to characterize Democratic Conventions… wholly disappeared."

RUNNING FOR OFFICE

THAT SAME YEAR—1883—Ben Johnson, editor of the *Wilkes-Barre Union Leader,* stood as a Democratic candidate for the office of Reading Clerk of the Pennsylvania House of Representatives. (The actual title was "Register of Wills.") In the run-up to the voting, newspaper support for him from both Democratic- and Republican-leaning publications was strong and widespread across many surrounding counties. A few examples:

- HAZLETON: *Mr. Johnson would make a capital clerk.*

- SCRANTON: *There is not a man in Luzerne better fitted for the position.*

Signs of the Times

- In 1876, Alexander Graham Bell was granted the first patent for the telephone, enabling the transmission of the spoken word and revolutionizing communications, initially via the Bell Telephone Company, which he established in 1877.

- In August of 1878, a new Lackawanna County, with its county seat Scranton, was carved out of Luzerne County, following decades of attempting to gain 'independence.'

- In 1879, Thomas Edison patented the electric light bulb in Menlo Park, New Jersey (following an improved stock market ticker in 1869 and phonograph in 1877, and before the motion picture camera in 1888).

- WILKES-BARRE: *Mr. Johnson is well and favorably known among all classes of our citizens. His political and journalistic career began as a firm friend of the workingman, and among this class of voters, Mr. Johnson would… draw heavily from the ranks of the opposing party. The press of the county—of all parties—both English and German, have spoken warmly of Mr. Johnson's candidacy.*

- SCRANTON (DEMOCRATIC): *Mr. Johnson would make an excellent Register…He would be elected. He would be the right man in the right place.*

- WILKES-BARRE (REPUBLICAN): *We believe that the Democratic party could not easily make a better nomination.*

- HAZLETON (INDEPENDENT): *Mr. Johnson is a gentleman of more than ordinary attainments…is one of the most generous men on earth and would be conscientious, honest and courteous in the discharge of his duty.*

- BROOKVILLE: *We know of no man in the State who would fill the position more worthily than Mr. Johnson.*

- DOYLESTOWN: *A more competent man cannot be found.*

- CATAWISSA: *No abler appointment could be made. It isn't salary, but honor we want, all newspaper men are millionaires, or ought to be.*

- WHITE HAVEN: *…his special fitness for the position. He has the ability to perform the duties of that office with credit to himself, and honor to the body that selects him.*

Other supportive editorials came from Philadelphia, Plymouth, Mahoning, Shickshinny, Bloomsburg, Warren, Sullivan, Bryn Mawr, and other regional newspapers.

After winning the position "several lengths ahead," the press remained positive in summing up the outcome:

- SCRANTON: *C. Ben Johnson...took no baits of anybody's contriving, but adroitly managed to gradually make himself a favorite with all the factions.*

- WILKES-BARRE: *Mr. Johnson has been a live-long worker for the interests of the laboring men, and his election to the position is a fitting recognition to them, as well as to the Democracy.*

FOUNDING THE BOARD OF TRADE

THE NEXT YEAR—1884—Ben was involved in establishing the Wilkes-Barre Board of Trade (BOT) for 'the encouragement and protection of trade commerce,' to be composed of 'individuals interested in the general prosperity of the city of Wilkes-Barre." These included most of the area's "banks and trust companies, mercantile and industrial establishments, lawyers, doctors, and leading influential business men"—that is, the city's commercial leaders and primary employers. And the membership included the anthracite mining companies and their owners and managers. From the beginning "special stress is laid upon advertising the advantages of the city as a place for home and business and the securing of domestic industries for it."

Signs of the Times

- In 1883, transcontinental railroad travel sparked the adoption of four standard time zones across the U.S. and Canada.

- In 1886, the American Federation of Labor is founded in Columbus, Ohio.

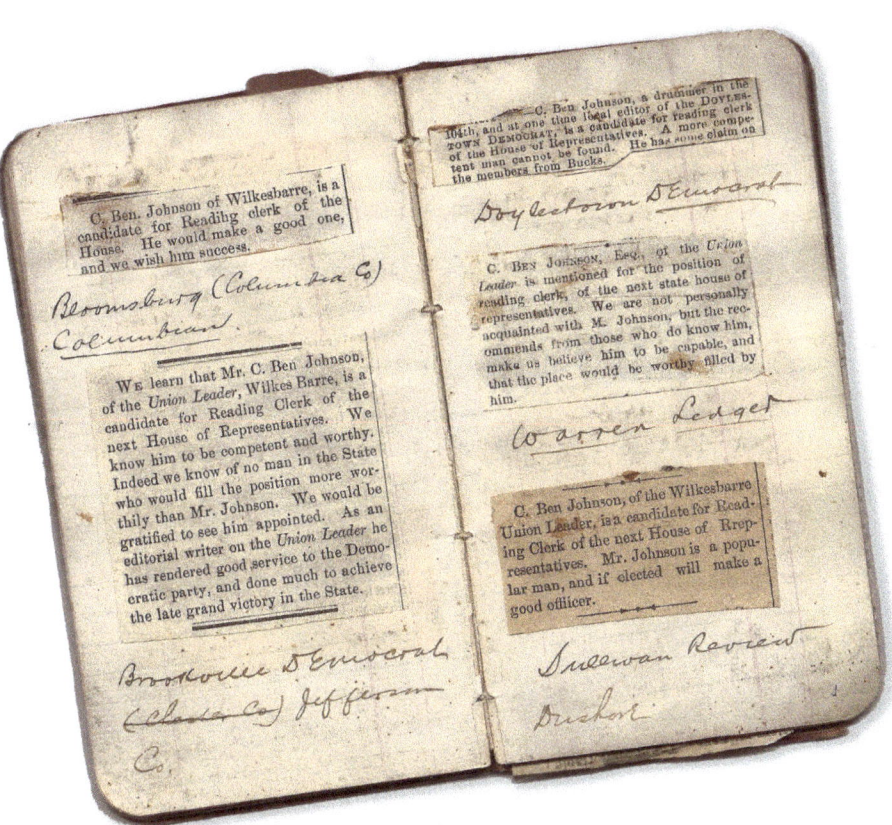

C. Ben Johnson's scrapbook of area newspaper endorsements and other comments on his candidacy for Reading Clerk of the Pennsylvania House of Representatives.

* * *

IN OCTOBER 1884, the Johnsons' nine-year-old daughter Gertrude was suddenly taken sick with diphtheria and died nearly a week later after a painful decline at home. Floral tributes included several from her schoolmates and neighborhood friends. A funeral was held also at home, and she was buried in Hollenback Cemetery.

* * *

By 1887, the Board of Trade's leadership had waned and when interest began to lag, a committee consisting of Hon. C. Ben Johnson, G. Mortimer Lewis, and Maj. C. N. Conyngham was appointed to refresh the BOT. They gave it new impetus, including fitting up rooms and naming Ben Secretary. The organization began to grow again, and membership "soon swelled" to 300. Ben Johnson remained Secretary for the next decade.

The BOT—which much later evolved into the Greater Wilkes-Barre Chamber of Commerce—was created with the goal of working to help area businesses succeed and grow. And it continued to do so for decades. An informative Board of Trade marketing booklet in 1906 referred to the city as:

Old in years but young in vigor!
and
Always alive, awake, alert and actively astir!

By that time—1906, twenty years after BOT's founding—Wilkes-Barre's industrial and commercial base was robust and diversified, with eight railroads running through the town: Pennsylvania; Lehigh Valley; Lackawanna; Erie; Central Railroad of New Jersey; Delaware & Hudson; Wilkes-Barre & Hazleton; and Lackawanna and Wyoming Valley. At least partially driven by the efforts of the Board of Trade, the industrial base had mushroomed and included a long list of companies in many different industries, including Sheldon Axle Company's Plant, First National Bank, People's Bank, Hazard Wire Rope Works, Raeder Printing Company, W-B Lace Mills, Matheson Motor Car Company plant, Adder Machine Company's factory, and Hess Goldsmith & Co.'s new silk mill. Most were moves or expansions from elsewhere, but some were manufacturing start-ups.

In 1893 the Wilkes-Barre & Eastern Railroad was built.
This short-route railroad traveled southeast out of Wilkes-Barre.

Reflecting on the 1880s establishment and growth of the BOT, and Ben's leadership, a newspaper editorialized that "Wilkes-Barre had its ideal Board of Trade. The secretary was C. Ben Johnson. At every meeting he had some prominent speaker and various diversions besides the routine business. He was a hustler of the most pronounced type. As a result of his secretaryship Wilkes-Barre acquired some industries that now are among the most substantial within our municipality. The members were enthusiastic and the large hall...was often too small to accommodate the outpouring of businessmen and others."

* * *

Ben received a letter, dated June 5, 1888, from the former Civil War General William Tecumseh Sherman at the Army Building in New York City. It read:

Army Building

New York, June 5, 1888
C. Ben. Johnson Esq.
Wilkes-Barre Pa.

My dear Sir:

I am indebted to you for your very interesting and expressive letter of the 2nd just with enclosure.

It is my intention to attend the National Encampment of the G.A.R. at Columbus, Ohio, about Sept. 10-12, when the subject you note will naturally be discussed. Meantime I prefer to limit my action to a simple suggestion of the propriety of the case, instead of indulging in answering a flood of correspondence which has begun to pour upon me.

With many thanks for your cordial expressions of regard I am

Very truly yours

W.T. Sherman, General

Although Ben's original June 2 letter to Sherman has been lost, we know that Ben remained connected and active with the G.A.R. some 25 years after the War, and his contacts and perhaps influence beyond the Wyoming Valley were well-developed. Sherman was a regular participant in the annual National Encampments, the September one in Columbus being the 22nd. Ben was an active leader at the G.A.R.'s Conyngham Post No. 97 and was its commander in 1890, when its "fine large Memorial Hall was being constructed."

> Army Building
> New York. June 5. 1888
>
> C. Ben. Johnson Esq
>   Wilkes-Barre Pa.
>
> My dear Sir:
>   I am indebted to you for your very interesting and expressive letter of the 2nd Inst. with enclosure. It is my intention to attend the National Encampment of the G.A.R at Columbus Ohio, about Sept. 10-17, when the subject you note will naturally be discussed. Meantime I prefer to limit my action to a simple suggestion of the propriety of the case, instead of indulging in answering a flood of correspondence which has begun to pour upon me. With many thanks for your cordial expressions of regard I am
>   Very truly yours
>   W. T. Sherman
>   General

General Sherman was a regular participant in the annual G.A.R. National Encampments, the September one in Columbus being the 22nd.

* * *

IN 1888 OR 1889, C. Ben Johnson served a short term as Secretary of Sanson Cutlery Co. The company was a significant manufacturer of knives and forks, which was absorbed by the Wyoming Cutlery Company in 1889.

* * *

IN THE FALL OF 1889, CBJ's mother, Mary G. Johnson, of Philadelphia, had been staying at Ben's house on South Franklin Street in Wilkes-Barre. Although she was 73 years old, she was "unusually active and of a merry disposition." On September 14, however, she suffered an "apoplectic stroke." And although regaining partial consciousness the next day and with full family and doctor care, she died four days later. Newspaper coverage of her demise refers to her as "the mother of C. Ben Johnson, Secretary of the Board of Trade," and another explains "while on a visit to her son, C. Ben Johnson, a brilliant newspaper man for many years connected with the Wilkes-Barre Leader." Such first page coverage signals the stature of the Board of Trade and Ben's role there and at the newspaper.

Ben's father, residing in Philadelphia, outlived his wife, but there is no indication that he visited or communicated with Ben or his family.

* * *

ON NOVEMBER 13, 1889, the G.A.R. put on an "Open Camp Fire" at the Wilkes-Barre Armory. Such patriotic community events were an ancient custom but had not taken place in recent memory. This inaugural night of a proposed series proved "brilliant and especially pleasant," with a large and enthusiastic audience made up of old soldiers and citizens. Local Post Captain Darte presided, gave a "stirring brief address" to open the proceedings, and introduced General Osborne as the senior military leader present. Following the General's speech, the entire crowd sang the old song 'John Brown's Body Lies Mouldering in the Grave' "with stirring enthusiasm."

> "C. Ben Johnson was next introduced and he quaintly referred to the fact that he wore no epaulettes during the war and stood in the galaxy of brilliant soldiers simply as a "high private."

> He then "launched forth in eloquent strains, apotheo-sizing the heroism of the boys in blue and enthusiastically defending them against the charge that they are paupers depending upon the Government. All did not want pensions. Those who came home maimed and crippled deserve it."

The choir then sang 'When this Cruel War is Over' "tenderly and effectively." Several long poems were read to finish off the evening.

Less than two weeks later, on November 24, Ben was speaker of the evening at a Sunday lecture event sponsored by the St. Aloysius Society, held at their hall in Wilkes-Barre. The talk was entitled "The Human Side of General George Washington." Preceded by seven vocal and guitar solos, Ben gave an amazing profile and assessment of Washington's personality, manner of balancing his priorities and dealing with his admitted shortcomings, and his constant doubts and insecurities. Drawing on Washington's many personal letters and many unknown or unusual anecdotes, Ben's commentary successfully proved that Washington was indeed but a man and not a god. However, flaws—tragic or otherwise—were not the point, and Ben closed with the sentiment written *"on a fly leaf of the bible on which General Washington took his oath of office as President":*

> *"Fame stretched her wings and with her trumpet blew,*
> *Great Washington is near, what praise is due!*
> *What title shall we give him? She paused and said:*
> *Not one; his name alone strikes every title dead."*

The hall was standing room only, the speaker frequently applauded, and he "sat down amid an enthusiastic clapping of hands." (Although the speech itself has been lost, a detailed contemporary summary of Ben's speech is contained in the Appendix 2.)

Ben's interest in these aspects of President Washington, and his research, insightful assessment, and orally striking and convincing presentation demonstrate the breadth of his interests and work, as well as the enthusiasm and respect held for him by his neighbors—and his impact on them.

Less than two weeks after that—on December 6, 1889—Ben delivered a 'paper' at a Board of Trade meeting suggesting a possible new mechanism for raising money to entice and help finance prospective manufacturers for Wilkes-Barre. His thinking was meant to address the fact that "The one thing the Board cannot do, as a Board, is to provide the requisite money." At the same time, he notes:

> *"When we say that 'money talks,' we may be fairly considered as having vulgarly expressed ourselves, but 'money talks' nevertheless. And it talks with especial directness and emphasis, and is about the only thing that does talk in that way, when the securement of new or enlarged industries for a city is the subject to be dealt with."*

The innovative money-raising scheme would allow individuals of even moderate and modest means to pool their savings through an Association, which would invest in the businesses that come to town. The investors would receive a rate of interest and, as partial owners, would receive additional returns as dividends after a year or two. Ben's purpose in suggesting such a scheme and structure was not to formally propose it but, rather, "to offer it as embodying what should give thoughtful citizens something to think about and as promising at least a possibility of results profitable to the whole community."

In his introductory remarks, Ben summed up the mission and central thrust of the Board of Trade that he had put in place and practiced over his first five years at the helm. In his words:

> *"The Board can and does persistently represent the city's advantages as an industrial centre to its own citizens and to outsiders. This, of itself, is no holiday job, and involves close application, constant watchfulness, and some little ingenuity in the devising of the easiest and cheapest means of accomplishing it.*
>
> *It is work, however, that in Wilkes-Barre has been sufficiently long in progress to have become fairly systematized, and the Board, therefore, can be depended upon to procure and produce, at short notice, the necessary data as to each proposed new industry or enlargement of an old one, with the evidence of its suitability to the locality, its probable prospects as a means of employing the idle labor of the city and vicinity, making money for the investors, etc., etc."*

A central theme and objective of the Board of Trade during Ben's tenure was to bring new manufacturing and other businesses to the Wilkes-Barre area and foster their expansion, including of their workforces. As the industrial base grew, and the Board remained aggressive in recruiting more, some resident companies raised eyebrows when attempts were made to lure their competitors. One of Ben's 'recruiting' initiatives was met with the following editorial encouragement: "C. Ben Johnson, Wilkes-Barre—Go ahead. We think you will act wisely if you get a couple of Lynn shoe factories to locate here. Never mind what rival concerns may say. Get all the factories you can."

A STINT IN THE PENNSYLVANIA HOUSE

BY YEAR-END OF THAT YEAR and into January of 1890, Ben began to be mentioned as a potential Democratic candidate for Congress—that is, for the district's seat in the House of Representatives in Washington. He was not actively seeking the nomination and in fact was not sure he wanted it, being either reluctant or coy. But early assessments by others were encouraging, actually glowing. For example:

> "Would be a popular candidate with all classes, by reason of his peculiar fitness for the position and great capacity for work."
>
> "Would make a working member, who might make speeches occasionally to let it be known that he can speak, but whose time would be occupied chiefly in quiet but persistent work for the people of the district."
>
> "He has a wider personal acquaintance, with both rich and poor, has the confidence of a larger percentage of both classes, and comes nearer in his convictions and writings to removing and harmonizing their differences, than any other man in the county."
>
> "His principles are now what they always have been, and I have never known him to hesitate to avow them, no matter in what presence."

"No other Democrat in the county can poll so large a labor vote, soldier vote, and the vote of capital as can Mr. Johnson."

"Mr. Johnson is a talented and energetic young man...well informed on all public questions, fearless in the right, bitter in denouncing and opposing wrong."

In February 1890, with the Democratic Congressional candidate still undetermined, an impressive letter of support for Ben was proffered by General W. W. H. Davis, who organized and led the 104th Pennsylvania Regiment throughout the War, 25 years before. In his comments, the General reveals a detailed and admirable profile of C. Ben Johnson as a soldier. Said Davis:

General W. W. H. Davis

"Mr. Johnson has another element of strength, he was a soldier in the war for the Union. In September 1861, when fifteen years old, he came to Doylestown and enlisted in Colonel Davis's regiment as a drummer, and served faithfully through a long enlistment. When there was no drumming to be done, "Charley," like the rest of the drum corps, took up the rifle, and met the enemy with his own weapon. Nominate him by all means—and send a drummer boy to Congress. "The Drummer Boy's Ticket" would be popular in the Valley of Wyoming."

This letter is revealing in several ways. It shows that Ben's profile and career in the quarter century following the Civil War was noticed and carried some weight with Davis, who at age 69 still owned and ran the Doylestown newspaper (among other things). It also conveys—and publicizes—Ben's role as a drummer boy in the Army, about which Ben rarely if ever commented, but from at least 1890 onwards was no secret. And the Davis testimonial is the only reference—or even hint—that C. Ben Johnson was ever addressed as 'Charley.'

An opinion poll in June of 1890 showed that the incumbent Representative in Harrisburg, George Stegmaier was far ahead in popularity and would be a shoe-in for re-election. He garnered 242 'votes,' and of the 13 others named, Ben was second with 15 votes. Shortly after the poll, however, Stegmaier decided not to run for re-election, with business pressures drawing him back to his family's large brewing company. This cleared the way for Ben's candidacy for the Pennsylvania House, and in the event he never ran for the Congressional seat.

In the midst of this summer of electioneering, Ben was the 'orator of the day' following a four-hour Fourth of July parade through Wilkes-Barre "under a blazing sun". The meeting at the Armory was attended by some two hundred men and was opened with a prayer and the reading of the Declaration of Independence. After quelling a distracting drum corps playing just outside the hall, Ben gave a "carefully prepared and well delivered" speech on the merits and accomplishments to date of "the government under which we live" and how it "tends to elevate the common man, make life worth the living to him and wipe out ignorance and poverty which are the fruitful sources of anarchy and rebellion." Poignantly:

> *He traced the wonderful progress of the nation during the one hundred and fourteen years of its existence; the gigantic enterprises that employ millions of dollars of capital and millions of men; the scientific discoveries that place her in that front rank of culture and intelligence.*

> *These are sources of pride and we should be proud of these achievements. But it is not in these that the chief glory of our country lies. It is in the lifting up and educating of the common men and women of our nation that is the crowning glory or our free institutions.*
>
> *He made an eloquent plea for patriotic sentiment in politics and condemned the narrow sectional strife that finds its way into political controversy. The boodler and the healer were scored unmercifully, and a strong stand taken for the purity of the ballot, the sacred birthright of the American freeman.*
>
> *He closed with an eloquent peroration upon the necessity of patriotism.*

As leader of the Board of Trade with great impact for more than four years, Ben had come to favor and support programs and legislation that were perceived to serve the companies, often mis-interpreted as to the detriment of the workers. This included opposition to several central and high-profile bills proposed by labor, namely the Night School Bill, the Two Weeks Pay Bill, the Employer's Liability Bill, and a statewide proposal to consolidate school systems.

Opponents portrayed Ben as anti-workingman. Just prior to the Democratic convention in August, 1890, for example, state senator and fellow Democrat W. H. Hines was quoted in a front-page newspaper article with a scathing personal attack citing Ben's tenure as House Reading Clerk some seven years before. Said Hines:

> *During the entire session, whenever he was in fit condition to talk, which was very seldom, he devoted his time in lobbying against our labor bills....He was several months*

absent from his desk during the sessions, and spent his time in such a way, and in such a place that if the same was ventilated during [this] campaign, should he be a candidate [for the house], no citizen with any degree of self-respect will vote for him....We will surely lose this district if the party is so unfortunate as to place him in nomination.

Nevertheless, at the 1st District (comprising the City of Wilkes-Barre) Democratic convention on August 25, Ben was indeed nominated for the Pennsylvania House seat, as was the Honorable J. Ridgway Wright, a former House member. Ben won that vote by 14 to 8 among the 22 delegates—"amid cheers."

The two-month campaign was marked by another flood of expressions of support and positive press articles in Ben's favor, despite a typically Republican electorate. In fact, one written by a Republican made the point:

C. Ben Johnson is a pronounced Democrat, but he would be one of the best representatives, would accomplish more for the city, and would more ably represent and look after the city's interest than would any other man who might be sent to Harrisburg...I am for C. Ben Johnson against all comers.

Another pointed to his able leadership:

Most assuredly, C. Ben Johnson, the able Commander of the Ely Post and the efficient Secretary of the Board of Trade.

And another, implying 'a man among men':

For Representative First District? C. Ben Johnson, from the bottom of my heart. The men in Luzerne County, possessing the brains and intelligence that C. Ben Johnson carries are few.

The newspaper editorials and campaigns against him proliferated following his nomination as the Democratic candidate. Some were strong:

> *The workingmen of this city are too well acquainted with his record at all times on labor issues.*
>
> *Whereas, C. Ben Johnson has been nominated by the Democrats for representative of the First District, through the influence and manipulations of a few prominent Republicans for sinister purposes of their own—among them the defeat of school consolidation; and*
>
> *Whereas, said C. Ben Johnson has been for over seven years past the bitter foe of all legislation intended for the benefit or elevation of the working classes; therefore be it*
>
> *Resolved, that we declare his nomination an insult to the workingmen of this city, and their interests demand his defeat.*
>
> *Resolved, that as the Republican candidate is also unsatisfactory to us, we deem it advisable to recommend the nomination of a workingmen's candidate.*

And the *Scranton Republican* predicted:

> *It is admitted on all hands that C. Ben Johnson will be the worst beaten candidate that ever has ran for the legislature in the Wilkes-Barre district. Johnson should have known better than to tempt fate. That seems to seal Johnson's fate.*

But competing newspaper *The Wilkes-Barre Times* offered support of Ben's record on labor issues and predicted the opposite outcome:

> The 'aristocratic affiliations' of C. Ben Johnson, so touchingly deplored by the Record, have been chiefly for the purpose of seeking opportunities for employment for labor and to solicit contributions for the relief of sufferers by disaster and misfortune.

> **Signs of the Times**
>
> • 1893 saw an economic panic that spurred a ten-year depression, with business collapses, unemployment that exceeded ten percent, and violent labor unrest.
>
> • The historic workers' strike at the Pullman Palace Car Co. in Chicago took place in 1894, requiring intervention by Federal troops and resulting in 34 deaths.

And *The Scranton Times* predicted a positive outcome:

> Mr. Johnson is practically certain to be elected by a handsome majority...as one of the comparatively few men who take interest and find enjoyment in the study of all that class of questions that affect the well-being of a community and involve political considerations.
>
> He has a great store of information regarding the rights and needs of labor, local taxation and municipal government, the influence of transportation monopolies in depressing industry and cruelly burdening the people, and he has the ability and the courage to make this information useful in shaping the legislation of the State.
>
> He will be supported in his candidacy by numbers of Republicans, because of these facts.

On election day, November 4, 1890, "though there were Republican, Prohibition and Labor candidates against him, Ben was elected by 239 votes." He carried 13 of the election districts, with the overall results:

CANDIDATE	PARTY	VOTES
C. Ben Johnson	DEMOCRAT	2,519
Robert W. Williams	REPUBLICAN	2,280
Jeremiah S. Sanders	PROHIBITION	241
S. S. Weller	LABOR	237

And, a month to the day after the election, Ben—then 43 years old—was re-elected as Commander of the G.A.R. Conyngham Post 97 (the 'Ely Post').

As a member of the Legislature from 1890 to 1892, he devoted much of his time to advocating for free schoolbooks, and for a bill making it a misdemeanor for candidates or political committees to pay the taxes of voters or the cost of naturalizing aliens.

He was widely respected and praised both in the run-up to the election and during his 1890-1892 term. But he did not stand for reelection after a single term. Although his reasons for not seeking to remain in office are unclear, perhaps he concluded that his impact would be greater in his home communities than in Harrisburg. He may have believed that his heart and greatest influence lay in journalistic advocacy rather than direct involvement in government and politics. Or perhaps work on national and local issues and time to do so were compromised by a full schedule in the capitol. Perhaps he didn't like Harrisburg, spending time there, and commuting. In any case, after his brief stint in the Pennsylvania House, he remained actively involved and a leader in Board of Trade and union activities and their organization and development in his home county.

WRITING, SPEAKING AND POLITICS

MAY 7, 1893, saw the birth of a granddaughter, Dorothy H. Innes, who would marry Arthur Turner and become the grandmother of this author.

In the fall of that year, Ben helped organize a new local institution for the treatment and cure of "the alcohol, morphine, opium, chloral, cocaine and tobacco habits." Named the Wyoming Valley Sanitarium and modeled after another such facility in nearby New York, it was located in downtown Wilkes-Barre in the winter, but patients spent the summers at a "suburban retreat." From its inception, Ben served as Secretary and General Manager.

By 1894, the booming U.S. economy and its thirst for immigrant workers to fuel the growth had turned into a severe recession with significant unemployment, low and declining pay levels, and continuing unacceptable working conditions in mining and other industries. (The Pullman strike in Chicago that summer had triggered strikes of 250,000 workers in 27 states.)

In April of that year, Ben was elected to Secretary of the Democratic County Committee—an important post in advance of the pivotal presidential election coming in 1896.

In the December 1894 issue of *The American Federationist*, Ben Johnson authored a hard-hitting piece, entitled "Close the Ports", in which he rebuked union leaders for having lacked the courage to advocate what they knew was in labor's best interest—that is, to disallow further immigration until the economy and job markets recovered and the 'oversupply' abated. Selections from Ben's precise and logical argument include:

> *The supreme call of the present hour is an immediate closing of our ports against any and all immigration, the embargo to*

continue until every American workingman, by which I mean every workingman in the United States, now out of employment, shall have been provided for.

The recent [immigrants], being in excess of the capacity of our industries...to provide them with steady and remunerative employment, are congested in our cities...living a life of miserable privation and poverty...

...the growth of industries to employ hundreds, and at the same time forcing the coming of thousands to be employed.

We have been keeping out competition for the employer for many years. Let us make a trial of a new scheme—that of keeping out competition for the employee.

We sympathize with the oppressed of the Old World, but we have a duty to perform for the oppressed of the New.

We are...in the position of any other asylum whose dormitories are full up, the limit of whose capacities in the line of its charitable work has been reached and which must close its doors against further comers until time shall make room for them.

That which has thus far filled our coffers and made us to prosper, is now having precisely the reverse effect.

Along with this strong argument, however, Ben emphasized the importance of—and his support for—immigrant labor:

We are ourselves, the whole 70,000,000 of us, either of foreign birth or within a few generations of it. The sources of our national wealth and greatness are threefold. First—God. Second—our form of government. Third—our immigrants. Up to a certain point we grew in both national and individual wealth in exact proportion as our immigration increased.

But, he said, in the face of depression and mass unemployment, there could be no alternative to closing the ports...hopefully temporarily: *"We would stop immigration in sheer self-defense."*

* * *

THAT SAME MONTH, April 1894, Ben gave a Eulogy at a Scranton Elks Lodge No. 123 meeting "to memory of its members who died during the year." Formed nationally in 1888 as the Benevolent and Protective Order of Elks (B.P.O.E.), the Wilkes-Barre Lodge had been established in 1889, and the Scranton Lodge later that year. Unlike the later Rotary, the Elks were from the beginning dedicated to charity. An active member of the Lodge, and always a serious if not impassioned orator, Ben was 'sermonesque' that evening and his comments brought out the best of both the Elks and the honored deceased. Selections from Ben's speech:

> *The primary purpose of Elkism is charity against which all its other purposes but lean as adjuncts or incidents.*
>
> *As Elks, we have no politics; no religion other than the religion of God. We have but one secret...the names of the recipients of such practical charity.*
>
> *We are not here after the manner of the stock obituary eulogist, to credit them in your ears with having possessed all the virtues in the calendar, and with having, therefore, been impossible men. They were but human, just like ourselves, and they had their faults. These we have 'written upon the sand.' They had also their virtues. These we have inscribed upon the tablets of love and memory.*

The greatest of their virtues was their devotion to the tenets of this order. We cannot forget that these, our dead, helped us rear the beautiful home that Elkism has secured to its contingent in this fair city.

A MOVE TO SCRANTON

Ben and Sallie moved to Scranton in 1895, but Ben's activities continued to span both Luzerne and Lackawanna counties as they had for three decades.

Shortly after moving to Scranton, in November of 1895, Ben proffered an idea at an informal meeting in the Board of Trade rooms. He suggested that several five- or six-story buildings could be erected in Scranton, with a dozen or more smaller businesses each employing up to 20 workers recruited to rent the spaces. The building would provide shared power, shafting, light and water to the tenant businesses. He cited New York and Philadelphia as already capitalizing on such shared workspaces and believed that lower operating and living costs might well lure many such operations to Scranton. Scranton's lower costs gave it the advantage over Wilkes-Barre.

Ben's commercial development ideas made the Scranton news.

There is no evidence that the idea was put to practice in 19th-Century Scranton. However, 115 years later, in 2010, growth of the approach was accelerated by the high-profile company WeWork and by many other industrial parks and real estate

PART THREE | 77

developers across the country.

* * *

IN A RINGING *Philadelphia Inquirer* endorsement of Ben's successful efforts to establish and lead the Wilkes-Barre Board of Trade, a 1902 editorial goes beyond the case for statewide boards and lauds Ben's character and ethics, in part as follows:

> *See what one man in the person of C. Ben Johnson accomplished for the city of Wilkes-Barre.*
>
> *For at least a generation we have never heard him talk about himself. But about the town he works for he talks and writes now as he used to talk about the old* Anthracite Monitor. *One of the first labor organs of the day, it was also one of the best. It could not have been otherwise with Johnson at its head. And Johnson gave the earliest of his matured years, if not the best to what he then wrote and believed, and his work was ably done.*
>
> *If he has changed his mind with respect to certain notions he then entertained we must respect him for the change. It proves that he had a mind to change.*

PART FOUR

Early Decline

A SIGN OF A HEALTH PROBLEM appeared abruptly on the third Saturday in December of 1898, when Ben was 51. He suffered a debilitating "paralytic stroke" as he entered his Scranton home, falling backward with his head hitting the flagstone. A doctor Fulton was called to the house and sent Ben to nearby Lackawanna Hospital. Although they at first feared the base of his skull had been fractured, that was not the case. He regained consciousness on Sunday afternoon but was only able to speak occasionally in a whisper. Sallie had been at daughter Mary's home, and when they arrived at the hospital the next day, Sunday, they were told that Ben was "steadily improving and would doubtless recover." Afterwards was it pointed out that for two or three days prior, Ben "had shown signs of approaching paralysis and had frequently complained of numbness in his head."

After three weeks in hospital, his condition improved slightly, with the abating of the partial paralysis of his right side, "but his mind still wavored." Sallie took him home, but after just two days determined that he indeed belonged in hospital. Dr. Thompson told her that "the place for her husband was in an insane asylum, where his brain could be treated." But the Wilkes-Barre Lodge of Elks sent another doctor to examine Ben, resulting in his being moved to the Elks' private hospital. The newspaper of the day opined that "His weakened and weakening condition are against recovery. Under the circumstances, Mr. Johnson will probably be taken to Danville at the earliest possible moment." (Danville was a state mental hospital, some 50 miles down the Susquehanna from Wilkes-Barre.)

In the event, however, only two weeks later his condition had "materially improved" and although remaining in the same hospital, he was "able to be about the place somewhat. He spends most of the time in reading the papers and his mind seem to be clear on all subjects except that he cannot be convinced that there is any such place as Scranton." *The Wilkes-Barre Times* goes on to say, "The story that Mr. Johnson was hopelessly insane and that he would be in a short while removed to the Danville asylum is vigorously denied."

On Monday, November 17, 1902, Ben collapsed on the Public Square, and had to be carried into the Thomas Harte drugstore,

> **Signs of the Times**
>
> • In 1902, the 140,000-member United Mine Workers carried out the 'Great Strike,' which was settled after nine months and President Theodore Roosevelt's intervention.
>
> • On June 16, 1903, Henry Ford formed the Ford Motor Company in Detroit, pioneering the first large-scale production line manufacturing company, and signaling use of the internal combustion engine to revolutionize travel in America and worldwide, as well as creating new demand for steel and adding significantly to the demand for petroleum-based fuel.
>
> • On December 17, 1903, Orville and Wilbur Wright achieved the first successful gas-powered airplane flights on the Outer Banks at Kitty Hawk, South Carolina, in their improved Flyer III, setting the stage for the revolution in fast, long-distance transportation of people and things.
>
> • Anthracite miner employment peaked in 1914 at 181,000.
>
> • Rapid growth of Anthracite production continued to climb rapidly, reaching its peak in 1917 at nearly 100 million tons.

Ben and Sallie Johnson

then on to the police station. Dr. Ahlborn brought him to consciousness and he was quickly on the road to recovery.

Soon after the Public Square incident in early 1903, 56-year-old Ben moved into the Dayton Military Home in Ohio—referred to as 'Old Soldiers' Home.' All involved no doubt concluded that this facility offered the best combination of medical care for his continuing or growing condition and an active living environment.

Established by President Lincoln in 1865 as the National Home for Disabled Volunteer Soldiers, the facility was built on a 355-acre farm, and contained residences and a hospital, and came to conduct a broad range of religious, intellectual and recreational activities. The number of residents peaked at more than 5,000 in 1897, and buildings on the campus numbered 132 in 1930, when the Home was consolidated into the Veterans Administration.

Ben's move to Dayton was permanent, and he ceased to have a public profile or life outside the Dayton campus. Wife Sallie remained in Wilkes-Barre but visited Ben regularly, staying at the Home Hotel there. About the same time Ben moved to Dayton—in January 1903—Sallie suffered an attack of 'grip' (now called 'influenza'), from which she recovered over two weeks of confinement at home in Wilkes-Barre. Her periodic visits to Ben in Dayton continued and she spent a few weeks there several times a year and often with her sister, daughter, niece, or other lady friend. By 1905, Sallie was contributing "men's clothing" to the local United Charities.

* * *

BEN JOHNSON DIED at the Old Soldiers' Home suddenly on Thursday, October 3, 1907. His death was "entirely unexpected, as it was generally believed that he was in the best of health." It was a great shock to his wife who was at home in Wilkes-Barre, having just returned from a three week visit with Ben in Dayton. Ben was just 60 years old, and in view of his decade-long history of occasional and sometimes serious attacks, the cause of death is assumed to be a stroke or heart attack.

The next day's local paper—the *Dayton Herald*—reported the death, noting "He had been here but a short time, but made many friends. As soon as notice of his death was received, Dayton Elks took steps to notify his relatives at Wilkes-Barre."

Sallie's niece went immediately to Dayton to take charge of shipping the remains home. Ben's body arrived at Wilkes-Barre on the Saturday Lehigh Valley Railway 3:05 PM train and was taken to his wife's home at 36 South Washington Street.

Sunday's funeral arrangements and services were overseen by the Conyngham G.A.R. Post No. 97 and the local lodge of Elks. At 2:30 in the afternoon, a viewing and service was held at Sallie's Wilkes-Barre home on South Washington Street, led by

Reverend Horace Hayden of St. Stephen's Episcopal Church. The cortege then traveled the mile and a half to Hollenback Cemetery for burial. The final service there was led by the G.A.R. chaplain. Both services were "largely attended, hundreds calling at the home..." and "an army of beautiful floral tributes attested in a measure the popularity of deceased." Taps were sounded on the bugle and a volley fired by a "firing squad" of eight men from the Post, as the remains were being lowered. There also were a flag bearer and six pall bearers, "all veterans." Impressive for a former drummer boy.

Sallie Johnson lived until 1943, mostly at 786 Market Street in Kingston, about a mile from the Market Street bridge from Wilkes-Barre. A few months before she died, Mrs. C. Ben Johnson sent a letter dated February 17, 1943, to this author's mother and father congratulating them on their recent marriage. Sallie was 86 and is buried adjoining Ben in Hollenback Cemetery.

C. Ben and Sallie Johnson's plot in Hollenback Cemetery, Wilkes Barre, PA.

PART FIVE

Epilogue

THE UNITED STATES had 15 different presidents during Ben's 60-year lifetime, demonstrating how rare re-elections were during the last half of the 19th Century. (Those presidents were Polk, Taylor, Fillmore, Pierce, Buchanan, Lincoln, Johnson, Grant, Hayes, Garfield, Arthur, Cleveland, Harrison, McKinley, and T. Roosevelt.)

This author notes the coincidence that C. Ben Johnson, my paternal great great grandfather, was born in 1847, only months before the birth that year of my maternal great grandfather, sea Captain George W. Dow. And Ben died in 1907, only two months before Captain Dow shipwrecked off the coast of England.

Although Ben was raised in Philadelphia before the War, the coal counties of Schuykill, Luzerne, and Lackawanna were his life's home, as he lived a decade in Tamaqua, 20 years in Wilkes-Barre, seven years in Scranton, before a final five years away at the Dayton soldier's home. His daughter and granddaughter married Wilkes-Barre men. The granddaughter's husband's military career took them away from Pennsylvania for many years, but they too always considered Wilkes-Barre their family home and moved back the last decade of their lives.

Ben had many interests, was a prolific writer on diverse subjects, with an earnest but low-key and agreeable personality. He never sought fame, notoriety, or the spotlight. His unselfish loyalty and hard work on behalf of his home communities, his political party, and the public good pervade virtually everything he did.

Ben Johnson was a member of myriad journalism, political, civic, governmental, and fraternal organizations and played leadership roles in nearly all of them, as either 'editor' or 'secretary.' He was a man of words and ideas for positive change, and these positions provided the opportunity and platform—and the *requirement* in many cases—for convincingly putting forth those words and ideas to members of his community.

During his lifetime—the second half of the 19th Century and immediately following the Civil War—critical segments of society in central Pennsylvania were growing in size and stature, and also were sorting out their relative roles, powers, and inter-relationships.

There were the new and growing industries and companies, beyond the long-standing and important mine owners and railroad companies. These legacy and new companies were owned, run, and represented in the community by wealthy, or soon to be wealthy, men. Ben was not a member of this group.

And, across the several counties and towns there were the 'founding families' who had lived there for generations; owned land, farms, and small businesses; were pillars of local religious groups and churches; and elected their leaders from among themselves. Ben, on the other hand, had come to the counties at age 20 and without wealth or local family or friends, so he was not a member of this group either.

After the War, there were the local Union Army veterans, led by former officers and decorated men, respected for their wartime ranks and accomplishments, and reinforced and sustained by the formation of 'fraternal' organizations, including the G.A.R. They initiated and led many commemorative, patriotic, and charitable organizations. As a teenage drummer boy in the Army, Ben was not automatically a recognized or prominent member of this group.

Then, finally, there was the exploding growth of immigrants, especially to mine coal, build railroads, and work in the mills and factories, comprising mostly Irish Catholics and Germans seeking better lives in America and fomenting for better working conditions and pay. Labor unions were spawned from these workers, evolving from the Workman's Benevolent Association to the National Miners Union during Ben's working life. Ben was not an immigrant, miner, Catholic, or union worker.

While the relative roles in society among these various groups and power structures were being sorted out over the decades, Ben—an 'outsider' to each group—was able to provide and exert constructive leadership to all of them and make a significant impact on his community.

CBJ's profile in history is relatively low and rarely referenced in the annals of the American labor movement. However, he was a central character at its birth and early development. His advocacy and proselytizing of the need for improvements and advances in worker well-being was an important contribution to the modernization of American industry as the industrial revolution, the dependence on immigrant labor, and the fight for worker rights and wellbeing took hold.

The way he set priorities and handled difficult and sometimes fiercely-contested trade-offs, illustrate his razor-sharp focus on the communal good. For example:

All he did was oriented toward making life better for people across his community.

He represented generational change, from the town fathers and older generation of land and business owners and Civil War officers and men, to the modernizing world of industry, coal, oil, and rail transportation, and the rapid expansion of commerce.

On the one hand, he helped found and was the leader of the Board of Trade with its industrial and commercial membership, and employer sponsorship. On the other hand, much of his journalistic and civic work was aimed at and supportive of worker, union, and Democratic Party causes.

He passionately shared union values and objectives concerning worker pay and working conditions. At the same time, he was rabidly anti-violence.

He drew respect, influence, and power, not from military rank or heroics, inherited wealth, business career wealth and power, or being on boards with top corporate executives but, rather, through constructive ideas and persuasive writing and speaking, and by leading institutions and organizations via 'secretary' positions. It made him an insider and far more influential than outsiders and many more-prominent insiders.

He never wavered from what he believed, proposed, or advocated, yet suffered few negative or critical reviews or disagreements among media or individuals (other than occasional political critics)—astounding, given his taking strong positions on virtually all the issues of the day.

Many leaders of the era made their marks and greatest accomplishments as they grew older, whereas Ben's life was cut short at age 60, and he made all his contributions in prior decades.

As *The Evening News* summed up shortly after he died, "He was a ready conversationalist, a clear writer, a polished speaker and a delightful companion. His impulses were all generous, his affections warm, and his heart like an open book. May we all fondly treasure him in loving remembrance."

APPENDIX I

MEMORANDUMS OF

Chas. B. Johnson

WHILE CONNECTED WITH

Co. D 104 P.V.

AUGUST 1861—MARCH 1862

I enlisted and was sworn in on the 31st day of August 1861 by Captain Rogers—Captaiin Co. A. 104th Pennsylvania volunteers, boarded at Orem's hotel, corner of Main & State Streets, Doylestown until September when the camp was formed and those already enlisted slept there. Co. I. Captain Duncan came to camp the same day. I was attached to a squad and placed under the command of Serjt. C. R. Whipple of Co. I. The company with which I enlisted. Through some cause or other the company to which I belonged got broken up and after making application to Col. Davis I was placed in Co. D. of Quakertown under the command of Capt. Jacob Swartzlander. I was very well pleased with this not wishing to return after having once enlisted in the service of my country.

Companies and recruits came in rapidly and our Regiment was soon far advanced in its formation—October 5th the Regiment marched to Damborough, Bucks Co. to a Union Meeting then being held at that place. Col. David and several others made speeches and on the whole it was a very interesting time. The place was about five miles and we thought it to be rather a hard march but we have since found out what hard marching is having had plenty of it to do.

October 1861 • Doylestown, Philadelphia, Washington D.C.

October 9th 1861. On the 9th the men drew their muskets and all seemed to be anxious to get where they could use them. On the 10th we drew caps. All thought they were soldiers now for a surety.

October 12th 1861. On the 12th I got a furlough for 4 days and left camp for Philadelphia in the morning on arriving there cordially and warmly welcomed by my friends and relations. I passed my time pleasantly during my stay in the city and while there I got my uniform.

When I returned to camp, the Regiment was absent at Hartzville where they were provided with a sumptuous dinner. Speeches were made by Gen. Jonathan Davis and Col. Marple and the boys had a pleasant time.

The ladies of Bucks County presented the regiment with a silk flag and Governor Curtin presented us with the State Colors and made a speech at the presentation. The regiment escorted the Governor to and from the cars with the band playing and Colors flying.

Our camp was named Camp Lacey. We lay here quiet and had very easy times until the 5th day of October when we had marching orders read to us on Dress Parade.

The next morning we were up long before daylight and after making immense fires by piling up all the rubbish of the camp and amusing ourselves in different ways, we started. This was about 8 o'clock. Got on the cars and went down to Philadelphia. We halted at the Union Refreshment Saloon and were treated to an excellent meal after partaking heartily of the tempting viands here placed before us. We continued our march out Prime St. to the Baltimore Depot. We left Philadelphia amid the waving of handkerchiefs and the 'Good byes" and "God Bless Yous" of our friends.

It rained some little in the daytime and very hard after night. We arrived at Baltimore at daylight on the morning of the 7th and marched through the streets to the Washington Depot and getting on the cars started for Washington. We reached this latter place about 2 p.m. and halted at a sort of a barrack called the Soldier's Rest. Here we had an apology for a meal in the shape of some coffee brought to us in Horse buckets, salt beef and a dry crust.

October 1861-March 1862 • Washington D.C.

About sundown we left to find a camping ground. This we found about four miles out of the city where we halted, built blazing fires and bivouacked for the night. We slept middling well for the first night without shelter, although there was a heavy frost and it was very cold.

October 8th we pitched our camp on a hill called Kalarama Heights. The country around this part is broken and hilly. The water here was poor. While here we passed our time by drilling, "reviews" & c. For amusement we had the Rock Creek for swimming. By and by we had orders to leave after a barracks had been built by carpenters and others of our own regiment under the charge of J. M. Carver on Meridian Hill to be called Carver Barracks.

We left Camp Davis joyfully at the prospect of getting in good winter quarters. The night of the 24th being Christmas Eve was passed very pleasantly the boys having received a number of boxes of eatables from homes of which to make their Christmas Dinner.

December 25th 1861. This was our first holiday we had passed in the army and we occupied it in moving into our barracks. In fact these comfortable was as acceptable to us as a Christmas present as anything else could have been. After the boys had all got suited in their bunks and had them all fixed up attention was turned to matters of enjoyment and boxes of eatables were opened and disappeared in a remarkably short space of time. Altogether the day passed very pleasantly considering the bustle and confusion we were in just coming into our new home.

While here Col. Davis had command of the Brigade. The principal part of the line (consisting of 104 P.V., 52 P.V., 56 N.Y.V.) and we were forever being reviewed or inspected. The regiment was here learned to drill and manouvre well under the excellent and oft repeated tuition of our field officers.

On the 21st of March we received orders to have three days rations cooked and be in readiness to march. The men were all in high spirits at the propsect of leaving but we were compelled to wait for the wagons. The Regimental expressed their disapprobation of this by playing the old air of "Wait for the wagon" as a kind of appeal to our officers to get us off.

March 1862 • Washington D.C.

On the 22nd many were disappointed by the arrival of orders countermanding the last ones for marching. The next day we had brigade drill for the first time and our brigade when drawn up in line of battle alone made a line three fourths of a mile long.

On the 28th we again received marching orders while the men were on brigade drill. They were immediately dismissed and by 3 p.m. we were on our road for Alexandria, Va. This was a fatiguing march for the boys. We arrived at a camping ground at about 9 o'clock and passed our second night of bivouacking. The night was bitter cold and it did not pass as pleasant as our first night.

The next day, March the 29th, we packed up and marched about one mile and encamped. There we undertook to make ourselves shelter from our Gun Blankets, boughs and in fact anything we could find. I visited Col. Goslines Regiment and seen some boys I had been acquainted with in the city.

We did not succeed well in our endeavors to make ourselves shelter and the heavy snow and rain that kept up all that day and night proved it very much to our own discomfort. However we passed the night as well as could be expected and in the morning early we were up and marching toward Alexandria.

We reached that place, marched to the wharf and got on board of the U.S.S. Constitution. Our whole brigade was packed on this vessel. Our regiment being on the upper deck and it raining and blowing very hard we passed a rather unpleasant night. The ship was top heavy and was continually going from one side to the other. Capt. Swartzlander and H. Rohr of our Co. fell overboard but were gotten out before drowning. In the morning of the 31st for this reason our regiment went ashore and after partaking of a hearty meal we got on board of the State of Maine. Here our quarters were very comfortable compared with those we lately occupied on the Constitution.

About 11 o'clock we started down the river. We had a good view of both shores and the interesting objects of each among which was Mount Vernon, the residence of Washington, and Fort Washington. On passing this place we were saluted with three cheers from the troops there and a tune from their brass band.

April-May 1862 • Newport News, Yorktown

We arrived at Fortress Monroe April the 2nd and getting off we marched a distance of eight miles within two miles of Newport News in a peach orchard and encamped. The peach trees in the camp were in full bloom and gave the camp a very picturesque appearance. The duty was principally drilling and picketing in the swamps.

On the 15th General Casey reviewed us at Newport News. The troops made a fine appearance. On the 16th we took up the line of march for Warwick Court House a distance of eighteen miles from Camp Ripley. This was a very hard march on the men and caused a great deal of straggling and the throwing away of a great many clothes. We pitched our camp in a wheat field.

The next day, the 17th we marched two miles and encamped in a swamp within five miles of Yorktown. On Easter Sunday the regiment was on Picket Reserve in mud and water up to their knees. The guards fired at each other but hurt no one.

On the night of the 29th we made a reconnaissance to in front of Yorktown under the Command of Gen. H. M. Naglee. The Brigade lost two men and wounded one of the eleventh Maine and one of the 56th N.Y. This is the first time our men were under shelling.

While we lay at this place which was called Camp Scott we had very poor rations. The camp was a very pretty one, the streets being cut out of a solid pine woods. We lay here picketing in front of Yorktown until May 4th when we had orders to clean up and prepare ourselves for inspection. Immediately after the inspection was over we received orders to march. Accordingly we started and soon reached the Rebel Forts at Yorktown which were empty with the exception of torpedoes and these were scattered about pretty plentifully.

From here we made a reconnaissance towards the James River, the Rebs efacuating as we advanced. On our return we proceeded after the army towards Williamsburg on our arrival to where our brigade was. We laid down and bivouacked for the night.

May 5th we were called up at daylight and proceeded onward and encamped or rather halted within a half of a mile of the battleground. We soon received orders to move again and after maneuvering around nearly all day we stood in line of battle all night shivering and drenched with rain and mud to the skin.

May 1862 • Ft. Magruder, Bottoms Bridge, Seven Pines

The next day, the sixth, we marched to Fort Magrauder and encamped. The other troops were engaged tending to their wounded and burying their dead. Numbers were brought here.

On the 8th we had review and brigade drill and on the 9th we marched ten miles and encamped in what was once a cornfield but nothing but the stalks now remained.

On the 10th we left here and marched to a place called Ropers Church a distance of ten miles and encamped. At night our Co. was on reserve picket.

The 11th was a very sultry day and we had nothing to eat which did not much improve our condition.

On the 12th we started about nine o'clock in the morning and were until 4 o'clock the next morning in reaching New Kent C. The distance of eighteen miles.

The next day, we, having had nothing to eat for the two or three preceeding days, some of the boys started the cry of "crackers," and all joined in the cry which soon brought our the, at that time, much needed article.

On the 16th we marched about eight miles. The roads were good and weather fair.

On the 17th the Co was on picket.

On the 18th we marched six miles to a saw mill on the R.& W.P.R.R. and encamped.

On the 19th we had a skirmish at Bottoms Bridge. The regiment was between the two artillery fires. There was one man of the 52nd P.U. wounded.

On the 20th we again marched about three miles and stopped to encamp when we were ordered to cross the Chickahominy Creek immediately, which we did being the first regiment to cross that stream and slept on our arms all that night.

The next day we went back to camp and laid there all that day and the 22nd and on the 23rd we made a reconnaissance across the Chickahominy and returned to the Rifle Pits, stacked arms and went back to our old camp for knapsacks. We god a couple of hours sleep here and again crossed the Chickahominy to the Rifle Pits where our arms were stacked. Took the arms and continued the march to a place called Seven Pines, about seven miles from the creek, and attacked the enemy's pickets.

May 1862 • Seven Pines

A brisk engagement soon commenced and Regan's Battery soon moved up and in the course of two or three hours put the Rebs to a complete rout. Co's A & B were skirmishing and Co's T & D acted as support. Capt. Groff Co, the then 1st Lieutenant was wounded in the breast by a six pound shot. Private Brown of Co. C killed & Corp. A. Thompson of Co. D severely wounded beside one or two others slightly.

After driving the Rebs about one mile we returned to the woods in which the engagement commnenced and encamped. This was the 24th of May.

The next day we marched one mile further and encamped for the night. On the 26th we were up and off before daylight. About daylight we passed our picket line. This was in light marching order. In the evening we returned for our knapsacks and again started off and encamped at a place called Fair Oaks in front of a large wood pile.

On the 28th the Rebs attacked our picket line but were driven back, one wounded Reb was brought it.

May 29th we moved a piece further to the right and fixed our camp on the Baltimore Road. The boys were at work making an abattis of felled trees to prevent the Rebs from charging on our camp. It rained after night.

On the 30th the boys were at work digging rifle pits near the picket line.

About 11 o'clock on the morning of the 31st the Rebs threw three shots over at us. About this time Lieutenant Washington of the Rebel General Johnson's staff was captured and brought in. He told that the Rebs intended attacking us that day. An orderly soon rode up and our regiment was immediately drawn up in line of battle and marched off about one half mile towards the picket line. Our pickets were soon seen coming out of the woods and whole columns of Rebs after them in hot pursuit. The fight soon began in good earnest and in the course of three or four hours, no reinforcements coming up, our men were compelled to retreat hotly contesting every inch of the ground.

May-June 1862 • Fair Oaks, Seven Pines, Bottoms Bridge, White Oak Swamp

The battle raged until dark when both armies stopped as if by mutual consent. We lost about half of the men we took into the fight in killed and wounded. Col. Davis was wounded in his right arm and breast. Maj. Gries was killed. Lieutenant McDowell of Co K was killed and Capt. Swartzlander, Co D, Corcoran, Co. G, Orein, Co. B, Lieutenant Ashenfelder, Co. H, Lieutenant Kephardt, Co. B were wounded. Co. E were on Picket and were all taken prisoners. This was one of the most bloody battles on record for the number of men engaged.

June 1st. Fresh troops attacked the Rebs today and compelled them to retreat. Our regiment was encamped at Seven Pines, the site or our fight on the 24th of the month. This day with the two succeeding ones we passed here in the woods in no very comfortable condition the men having mostly all lost their blankets and other things in the fight.

On the 4th we were marched back to the Chickahominy. On account of the late heavy rains (for it had rained nearly all the time for the last week) we were compelled to wade through water waist deep which was rising at the rapid rate of about one foot in five minutes. However, we all got through safe and encamped at the Rifle Pits near the creek. At this camp our rations were very poor especially at first, nearly all our crackers were mouldy and this constituted the biggest half of our rations.

We crossed the Chickahominy and fixed our camp at Despatch Station on the line of the R & W P.R.R. We lay here quietly until June 28th (rumors of Jackson's Raid had been coming in for the last few days and we had heard heavy firing on the right) when we went again across the Chickahominy and threw up the Rifle Pits around Bottoms Bridge.

This position we held for two days with the help of a few pieces of field artillery. On the 28th the Rebs undertook to shell us from the other side. But one of our field pieces soon stopped their gabbling by putting a few shots over at them.

On the evening of the 29th we left here and halted at the White Oak Swamp Bridge.

June-July 1862 • Harrison's Landing, Williamsburg, Yorktown

The next day, June 30th, there occurred one of the heaviest artillery fights ever heard of. We were under their fire all the forenoon but none were hurt. The next morning at one o'clock we left and on the march there occurred what is known as the Mill Charge, a scene which can be better imagined than described.

July the 2nd we had a skirmish at Carter's Hill and were guarding the wagon train we had been Rear Guard of the army ever since it left the Chickahominy. We marched to Harrison's Landing on the 3rd. The regiment was on Picket.

On the 4th, Gen. McClellan reviewed the whole army. We soon ahd our camp established here within a short distance of the James River. The duty was pretty hard of the men being mostly Picketting. At times when Gen. Peck had the men out on Division Drill, he worked the men so hard that many dropped from the effects of the heat sun which at this season of the year in this climate is almost like an oven. Some one or two died from the effects of it. At such times it was whispered that the Gen. had been indulging in something stronger than water.

One night the Rebels opened forty pieces of artillery on us from the opposite side of the river but our Gun Boats soon put a stop to them.

On the 15th, we had our knapsacks loaded on a canal boat and left camp in light marching order and marched about one or two miles and then had to return to camp again. That night we had a sham Dress Parade and built "stuffed paddies" and posted them as sentinels on the ramparts of the Rifle Pits we had built while there. I can imagine the Rebs stealthily advancing on their harmless foes after we had evacuated that place.

The next morning, the 16th, we left camp and marched 16 miles toward Williamsburgh and encamped in a large cornfield and in the maming of the 50 acres or more of flourishing corn that was there the day before. Nothing but a stray stalk here and there remained.

On the 17th we marched to within six miles of Williamsburgh crossing the Chickahominy, at its mouth, on the road a distance of twenty three miles. This was a very hard march, the dust being thick and the rations very poor.

On the 18th we started before daylight and passed through Williamsburgh to within seven miles of Yorktown, a distance of eleven miles.

July-November 1862 • Yorktown, Gloucester Point

On the 19th we all went on Picket. And having received permission to forage and we soon had plenty to eat. Beef, pork, fruit and in fact anything we could lay our hands on. The beef tasted good although it was roasted or rather smoked on sticks and eaten without salt.

On the 20th we marched through Yorktown and about three or four miles further and were just preparing for the night when we got orders to return to Yorktown, which we did, and got on board of the steamer Mystic and crossed to Gloucester Point on the opposite side of the York River. We bivouacked on the outside of the Fort at that place.

The next day we went inside of the Fort and put up a very comfortable camp from the shelter tents we had with us and boards, of which there was a goodly quantity to be had.

On the 24th we made a reconnaissance towards Gloucester Court House, marched about eight miles and encamped for the night in or near the road.

The next day the boys ransacked a Regel Colonel's house that stood near5 where we laid all night. We took chickens, ducks, geese, turkeys, watermelons and in fact everything in the eating line we could lay our hands on and in the evening returning nearly every man was stocked with eatables enough for a while at least. We brought back a doctor who was suspected to be a Reb but he was afterwards released.

On November 16th the darkies brought in the report that the Rebels were advancing on our Picket Line. Our Co. were immediately sent out as a Picket Reserve. Lieutenant L. H. Markley took ten men and went out as far as the Hook Store about one mile from our picket line and posted them in the edge of a woods. A squadron of about 60 cavalrymen soon made their appearance and were challenged by our men for a reply. They poured in a volley from their carbines and pistols killing P. Baltz and wounding A. Hilley, H. Trumborvey and Geo. Geary all of Co. D. Ser jts T. Leapherberry, L.A. Rosenberger and Private H. Shelley were taken prisoners. Our men returned to the picket line and the cavalry skedadled.

The next day the detachment of cafvalry that we had sent out the night before returned with a few prisoners. We drew Sibley tents and made a pretty as well as comfortable camp out of it by stockading the tents. The drummers tented together while here and we had pleasant times. We left the fort in a great deal better condition than it ever had been before and better than it is now I'll warrant.

December 1862-February 1863 • Gloucester Point, Carolina City, Hilton Head, St. Helena Island

But all good times must have an end and we were very sorry to leave, which we did on December 28th and embarked on the sailing vessel Wm. Woodbarry. The tug Jas. J. Treeborne towed us to Fortress Monroe on the 29th. On the 30th she towed us from Fortress Monroe past Cape Henry. It was stormy and continued so until January 2nd when we anchored off the Bar at Beaufirt Isle.

On the 3rd, which was the next day we disembarked and landed at Morehead City and marched three miles up the Newberne Railroad and encamped at Carolina City on the banks of what is called Boque Sound. The city is beautiful large place and consists of the Justice's and Shoemaker's house both in one, a rail road depot, a barn, stable and pig pen. During our stay at this place the weather was rainy and windy and very cold. The wind blew the dust awfully making it very disagreeable.

January 21st—In the morning about 8 o'clock we left our camp and marched down to the wharf at Morehead City and got on board of the U.S.M.S. Cahawba. *The next day was an eventful day for our boat. In the first place in endeavoring to get off we got on a sand bar and occupied nearly all the morning getting off after which we steamed down the harbor and anchored in front of Fort Macon. During that day and night we run into and damaged the steamer* Expounder & N. England *by running into a gun boat after night. Damaged our own wheel house considerable.*

On the 25th we moved to the mouth of the harbor and on the 29th left it altogether. We steamed all day and night and the next day and night on the 31st arrived off Hilton Head. We lay in this harbor until the 2nd when we went up the Broad River to Beaufort for coal and water. Here the Regiment disembarked on the 3rd and encamped outside of the town.

On the next day, the 4th, we again got on board of the Cahawba *and on the 5th sailed back and rejoined the remainder of our fleet at Hilton Head.*

We attempted to land on the 8th but after about three parts of the regiment got ashore we got orders to return to the vessel, which we did and on the 10th we got fairly landed on St. Helena Island.

On the 18th we were reviewed by Gen. Naglee.

APPENDIX II
The Human Side of General George Washington

A DETAILED ACCOUNT of C. Ben Johnson's address at the St. Aloysius Society, Wilkes-Barre, Pennsylvania, on November 24, 1889, as reported in *the Wilkes-Barre Times Leader, The Evening News*, Monday, November 25, 1889, page 1. The article:

The address of the evening was by C. Ben Johnson, entitled "The Human Side of General George Washington."

Mr. Johnson's treatment of his subject was somewhat novel and designed to enforce a point of much importance, though not usually so considered. Taking the data from the published letters of Washington, he showed

- *that, with all his ambition and opportunities, he was, even when honors seemed to be crowding upon him, much dispirited and doubtful of himself and disposed to complain of comparatively trivial inconveniences or losses he had suffered.*

- *That he was very extravagant in his tastes and yet scrupulous in looking after his due, and so desirous of gain that he bought lottery tickets and looked after the drawings, too.*

• That the constant use of the word fashionable in letters ordering supplies for his person and home and examination of the niceties and delicacies with which he was wont to surround himself even on the march and in camp, would probably have resulted in these days in his being called dudish.

• That he was, before marriage, in the habit of falling in love with every pretty girl he met, and wrote poetry addressed to them, and frightful doggerel at that.

• That he was guilty of many inconsistencies as between his advice and his practices, and that in many ordinary things which the speaker specifically detailed, he showed himself to be, in ordinary things, but an ordinary man.
Mr. Johnson's point was that it was so with all great men. When men cease to have the weaknesses of men, they cease to be men and become gods. Those things in which Washington was entitled to be thus criticized, rendered him, not less, but all the more the great man and hero, since it was demonstrated that when duty called and opportunity offered he could forget the man and rise almost to sublime heights. The fact that all men are more or less influenced by the weaknesses, the selfishness, the passions and prejudices of common humanity, should make us more tolerant of such faults, lest we discourage and kill the heroic instinct that might otherwise make even the humblest and least promising among us, heroes, should occasion offer.

Mr. Johnson's address was enlivened by several anecdotes of an amusing character and closed with an endorsement of the sentiment conveyed in the lines written on a fly leaf of the bible on which General Washington took his oath of office as president:

Fame stretched her wings and with her trumpet blew,
"Great Washington is near, what praise is due!"
"What title shall we give him?" She paused and said:
"Not one; his name alone strikes every title dead."

The speaker was frequently applauded and sat down amid an enthusiastic clapping of hands.

BIBLIOGRAPHY

GENERAL

American Federationist. The. Edited by Samuel Gompers. Washington D.C.: AFL-CIO, American Federation of Labor, October 1898, p. 165.

Aubrecht, Michael. *The Long Roll.* Fredericksburg, Virginia: pinstripe press, 2019, page 39.

"A United Board of Trade." *The Colliery Engineer.* [City?], August 1888, page 22.

Bucks County Civil War Library and Museum, Gorden Alley, 32 N. Broad, Doylestown.

City of Wilkes-Barre Pennsylvania, The (booklet). Wilkes-Barre, Pa.: Board of Trade, Raeder Press, 1906.

Fischer, William Jr. *104th Pennsylvania Infantry Regiment, The "Ringgold Regiment."* Scranton, Pa., October 20, 2009 and June 16, 2016.

Greeley, Horace. Letter to C. Ben Johnson (unpublished). New York, December 3, 1871, Turner family collection.

Harvey, Oscar J. *History of Wilkes-Barre.*

History of the Iron and Steel Industry in the United States Wickipedia entry

Johnson, C. Ben. Civil War Diary (unpublished). Bucks County, Pa., August 1861—March 3, 1862, Turner family collection.

Johnson, C. Ben. *Sketch of the Wyoming Historical and Geological Society of Wilkes-Barre,* (reprinted from the Sunday News Dealer Christmas Edition, 1880 [dense 5 pages].

Johnson, C. Ben. Scrapbook of press clippings regarding 1883 Reading Clerk election (unpublished). Wilkes-Barre, Pa., 1883, Turner family collection.

Johnson, C. Ben. "Close the Ports", *The American Federationist.* Edited by Samuel Gompers. Washington D.C.: AFL-CIO, American Federation of Labor, December 1894, pp. 216-7.

Kenny, Kevin. *Making Sense of the Molly Maguires.* [Place/date/publisher?] Pp. 123-126.

Machinists and Blacksmiths International Journal, Vol. IX, No. 11. Cleveland, OH: September 1872, p. 778.

Sandler, Martin W. *Immigrants.* New York: Eagle Productions, Inc., 1995.

Sherman, W.T. Letter to C. Ben Johnson. New York, June 5, 1888, Turner family collection.

Smith, S.R. *The Wyoming Valley in 1892.* Wilkes-Barre, Pa.: The *Scranton Republican* Print, 1892.

Smith, S.R. *The Wyoming Valley in the Nineteenth Century.* Wilkes-barre, Pa.: Art Edition, Wilkes-Barre Leader Print, 1894.

Sylvis, James C. *The Life, Speeches, Labors and Essays of William H. Sylvis (Late President of the Iron-Moulders' International Union; and also of the National Labor Union).* Philadelphia: Claxton, Remsen & Haffelfinger, 1872, p. 97

NEWSPAPERS, MOSTLY VIA NEWSPAPERS BY ANCESTRY AT HTTPS://WWW.NEWSPAPERS.COM

Dayton Daily News, The. Wednesday, September 28, 1904, page 14.

Dayton Herald, The. Friday, October 4, 1907, page 8.

Philadelphia Inquirer, The. "Personal Notes." September 21, 1889, page 4.

Philadelphia Times, The. "The Long Strike." June 11, 1875, page 1.

Record of the Times, The. Saturday, May 4, 1878, page 4.

Scranton Tribune, The. Thursday, 28 November, 1895, p. 3.

Scranton Wachenblatt, The. Thursday, October 10, 1907, page 5.

Sunday Leader, The. Sunday, November 2, 1890, page 2.

Sunday News Dealer, The, Christmas Edition, 1880. Article re Wyoming Historical and Geological Society of Wilkes-Barre.

Union Leader, The
   Thursday, February 14, 1878, page 2.
   Thursday, September 26, 1878, page 3.
   Thursday, October 31, 1878, page 3.

Wilkes-Barre News, The
   Friday, July 18, 1890, page 2.
   Tuesday, August 19, 1890, page 1.
   Thursday, April 20, 1905, page 8.

Wilkes-Barre Record, The
    Tuesday, August 26, 1890, page 5.
    Saturday, September 20, 1899, page 8.
    Friday, May 6, 1904, page 10.

Wilkes-Barre Times, The
    Monday, December 19, 1898, p. 6.
    Monday, January 16, 1899, page 5.
    Monday, Feb. 6, 1899, page 5.
    Tuesday, November 18, 1902, page 3.
    Friday, January 23, 1903, page 5.
    Monday, February 27, 1905, page 2.
    Friday, October 4, 1907, page 12.
    Saturday, October 5, 1907, page 7.
    Monday, October 7, 1907, page 2.

Wilkes-Barre Telephone, The
    Saturday, October 4, 1890, page 2.

Wilkes-Barre Times Leader, The
    Wednesday, September 17, 1902, page 8.
    The Evening News, Saturday, February 2, 1878, page 4.
    The Evening News, Thursday, October 30, 1884, page 1.
    The Evening News, Monday, November 25, 1889, page 1.
    The Evening News, Saturday, July 5, 1890, page 5.
    The Evening News, Monday, October 27, 1890, page 2.
    The Evening News, Saturday, September 30, 1893, page 8.
    The Evening News, Monday, December 2, 1907, page 9.

ILLUSTRATION SOURCES

iii (Drum) Musselman Library, Gettysburg College.
vii (C. Ben Johnson photo) Turner/Scott family collection.
xiv (C. Ben Johnson photo) 1892 Wyoming Valley Pics11.
6 (C. Ben Johnson photo) Turner/Scott family collection.
10 (C. Ben Johnson photo) Turner/Scott family collection.
12 (Diary pages) Turner family collection.
14 (Company D campaigns map) Turner family collection/Carpenter.
19 (Peninsula campaign map) Turner family collection/Carpenter.
20 (*State of Maine* photo) Mathew Brady, U.S. National Archives
23 (Howitzers photo) Library of Congress.
27 (Charleston campaign map) Turner family collection/Carpenter.
28 (*Cahawba* photo) Steamship Historical Society of America.
30 (Shenandoah campaign map) Turner family collection/Carpenter.
31 (Shenandoah photo) fineartamerica.com
32 (Company D poster) Worthpoint, accessed at http://www.worthpoint. com/wortho pedia/civil- war-illustrated-roster-104th-pa-1735543190.
34 (Doylestown monument) Historical Society of Pennsylvania.
37 (Conyngham G.A.R. Post 97 Memorial Hall) Luzerne County Historical Society.
35 (G.A.R. medal) Wikipedia, accessed at https://upload.wikimedia.org/ wikipedia/Commons/7/74/Grand_Army_of_the_Republic_medal.svg.
40 (Anthracite coal fields map) The Hopkin Thomas Project, accessed at thehopkinthomasproject.com.
46 (Greeley letter) Turner family collection.
48 (Greeley stamp) Accessed at usstampgallery.com.
49 (Sallie Johnson photos) Turner/Scott family collection.
52 (Wilkes-Barre photo) Luzerne County Historical Socaity
57 (Scrapbook) Turner family collection.
59 (Locomotive photo) Monroe County Historical Association.
60 (Sherman stamp) Accessed at usstampgallery.com.
61 (Sherman letter) Turner family collection.
67 (Davis photo) Accessed at https://www.findagrave.com/memorial/20185426/william-wattshart-davis.
77 (News clipping) *Scranton Tribune*, November 28, 1895, page 3.
81 (CBJ and Sallie photos) Turner/Scott family collection.
83 (Tombstones) John Kastendieck, Caretaker, Hollenback Cemetery, Wilkes-Barre, Pennsylvania.

INDEX

19th century 1
104th Pennsylvania Volunteer Infantry Regiment v, 7, 8, 15, 16, 18, 24, 26, 28, 30-32, 34, 67, 89, 103, 06, 107
786 Market St., Kingston, Pennsylvania 83

A
African Americans 4
Aiken's Landing 30
Alexandria, Virginia 19, 20, 29, 92
American Federationist 74, 103
American Federation of Labor 56, 103
American Legion 35
Ancient Order of Hibernians (AOH) 41
Annapolis, Maryland 30
Anthracite Mining v, 39
Anthracite Monitor 38, 42, 78
apoplectic stroke 62
Appomattox, Virginia 29
artillery 16, 21, 23, 24, 94, 96, 97

B
Baltimore Depot 17, 90
Battery Pringle 28
Battle of Bull Run 5
Battle of Wilson's Creek 5
Beaufort Isle 26
Bell, Alexander Graham 54
Bermuda Hundred, Virginia 29
Black Thursday 43
Black veterans 36
Board of Trade, Wilkes-Barre (BOT) vi, 56, 58, 59, 62, 64, 65, 69, 70, 73, 77, 78, 87, 103

Boque Sound 26, 99
Bottom's Bridge 21
Bucks County, Pennsylvania 5, 7, 8, 11, 30, 34, 90, 103

C
Cahawba 26, 28, 99, 106
California, 1848 gold rush 2, 5
Camp Lacey 5, 8, 31, 90
Carolina City 26, 99
Carter's Hill 24, 97
Carver Barracks 18, 19, 91
Carver General Hospital 19
Carver, Lieutenant 18
Catholics, Irish 86
Charlestown, Siege of v
Chesapeake Bay 30
Chickahominy Creek 21, 23, 94
Civil War vi, ix, x, xi, 3, 4, 12, 15, 30, 32, 33, 36, 59, 68, 85, 87, 103
Close the Ports 74, 103
coal v, 38
coal fields of Pennsylvania 40
coal mining 2, 3
Company D 104 Pennsylvania Regiment 6, 8, 9 16, 25, 26, 32, 106, 107
Confederate Army 9
Confederate States of America 4
Congress 33, 36, 42, 66, 67
Constitution 4
Constitution, U.S.S. 19, 22
Conyngham, Maj. C. N. 58
Curtin, Governor Andrew 5, 17, 90

D

Daily Union Leader 52
Danville asylum 80
Davis, Colonel W.W.H. 5, 17, 18, 27, 28, 31, 67
  General 67
Davis, Jefferson 4
Dayton Herald 82, 104
Dayton Military Home, Dayton, Ohio 81
Declaration of Independence 4, 68
Decline vi, 79
Delaware River 3
Democratic County Convention Committee for Luzerne County 54
Democratic Party 35, 87
Diamond City 53
District of Columbia 4
Dow, Captain George W. 84
Dow, Mary E. x
Doylestown, Pennsylvania 5, 7, 8, 11, 31, 34, 36, 38, 55, 67, 68, 89, 90, 103, 106
drummer boy(s) ix, xi, xiii, 7, 11, 67, 68, 83, 86
drumming 9, 11, 67

E

Eastern Pennsylvania 3
Edison, Thomas 54
Eight Hour Movement 45, 47
Elkism 76
Elks, Benevolent and Protective Order of Elks (B.P.O.E.) 76
Elks Lodge No. 123, Scranton 76
Employer's Liability Bill 69
Enterline, Edward 48, 49
Enterline, Michael 48
Enterline, Sallie J. x, 48

F

Fair Oaks, Virginia 16, 22, 95, 96
Fell, Jesse 39
financial policy 51
Fort Magruder 21
Fort Monroe 19, 20, 26, 29
Fort Sumter 26
Fort Wagner 16, 27, 28
Fort Washington 20, 92

G

Georgetown 17
Germans 86
Gloucester Point 25, 98, 99
Gowen, Franklin B. 43
Grand Army of the Republic (GAR) v, 31, 33
G.A.R. National Encampment 36, 60
G.A.R. Post No. 97's Memorial Hall 37
Greeley, Horace ix, 45, 46, 48

H

Harper's Ferry, West Virginia 29
Harrisburg, Pennsylvania 5, 29, 51, 68, 70, 73
Harrison's Landing 24, 97
Hayden, Reverend Horace 83
Hilton Head Island 28
Hines, W. H. 69
Hollenback Cemetery 57
Home Hotel, Dayton, Ohio 82
Howitzers 23, 106
Human Side of General George Washington, The 63, 100

I

immigrant labor 75, 86
immigration x, 74, 75
Industrial Advocate 51
industrialization 3
Industrial Revolution x
Innes, Dorothy Howard x, 74
Innes, Edgar A. x
Irish workers 41

J

James Island 27
James River 21, 24, 29, 30, 93, 97
Jas. J. Treeborne 26, 99
John Brown's Body 63
John's Island 27
Johnson, C. (Charles) Ben i, iii, iv, v, vi,
 vii, ix, x, xi, xiii, xiv, 2, 6, 7, 10, 11, 12,
 35, 46, 48, 49, 53, 56, 57, 58, 59, 62,
 63, 66, 67, 68, 70, 71, 72, 73, 78, 83,
 84, 100, 103, 104, 106
 as editor 38, 44, 49, 50, 54, 85
 as secretary 59, 85, 87
 Civil War diary ix, xiii, 11, 12, 13, 15,
  16, 89-99
 Memorandums about 89
Johnson, Charles Benjamin ix, xiv, 6, 7
Johnson, Gertrude Craige 50
Johnson, John Marion 7
Johnson, Mary Eva x
Johnson, Mary Guilliam 7

K

Kalorama Heights 17
Kehoe, John 42, 43

L

Labor Reformer 42, 50
Lackawanna County 54
Lackawanna Hospital 79
Lake Erie 3
Langdon, Frank W. 41
Lehigh Valley Railway 82
Lenape Native American 39
Lewis, G. Mortimer 58
Lincoln, Abraham iii, v, 4, 5, 7, 29, 81, 84
Logan, General John A. 33
Lutheran church 48
Luzerne County Historical Society xiii,
 106
Luzerne County, Pennsylvania xiii, 4,
 39, 50, 53, 54, 71, 106

M

*Machinists and Blacksmiths
 International Journal* 48, 103
Maine 4, 18, 19, 93, 106
Maine, State of 19, 20, 92, 106
Malvern Hill 23
manifest destiny 2
manufacturing 2
marching 15, 16, 17, 19, 89, 90, 92, 95, 97
Martinsburg 29
Mauch Chunk 43
McClellan, General 24
Memorial Day v, 31, 33
Meridian Hill 18, 91
Miners' Association of the Anthracite
 Counties 50
minimum age for military service 8
Missouri 4, 5
Missouri Compromise 4
Molly Maguires 41, 43, 44, 103

money talks 64
Morehead City, North Carolina 26
Mount Vernon 20, 92
musicians iii, 7, 11, 26
Mystic 25, 98

N
National Home for Disabled Volunteer Soldiers 81
National Labor Union 38, 42, 104
Native Americans 1, 3
Negro veterans 36
New Kent Center 21
Newport News 20, 93
newspaper endorsements 57
New York Tribune 45
Night School Bill 69
Norfolk 29

O
Old Soldiers' Home 81, 82
Orem's Hotel 8

P
paralytic stroke 79
patriarchy x, xi
Peck, General 24
Peninsular Campaign v, 19
Pennsylvania v, vi, ix, x, 3, 5, 6, 7, 8, 16, 18, 29, 34, 38, 39, 40, 49, 51, 54, 57, 58, 66, 67, 68, 70, 73, 84, 85, 89, 100, 103, 106
Pennsylvania Auditor General 51
Pennsylvania House of Representatives ix, 54, 57
Pennsylvania State mental hospital, Danville 80

Penn, William 3
Petersburg, Virginia, Siege of 16
Philadelphia v, 3, 4, 5, 7, 11, 17, 29, 30, 38, 42, 43, 56, 62, 77, 78, 84, 90, 104
Philadelphia Inquirer 78, 104
picketing 20, 24, 93
pickets 16, 21, 22, 94, 95
Pinkerton, Allan 43
Pittsburgh, Pennsylvania 5, 39
politics x, 13, 33, 35, 69, 73, 76
Portsmouth 29
Potomac 19, 29
Pottsville 43, 48, 49, 50, 52
Pottsville Chronicle 52
Pottsville Workingman 50
Powell, Morgan 43
Pullman Palace Car Co. 72
Pullman strike 74

Q
Quakertown, Pennsylvania 7, 8, 89

R
rations 15, 21, 24, 91, 93, 96, 97
Reading Clerk of the Pennsylvania House of Representatives ix, 54, 57, 69, 103
Rebs 21, 22, 24, 93, 95, 96, 97
Reconstruction 35
red eye 18
Republican Party 35, 36, 45, 46
Revolutionary War 5, 39
Richmond, Virginia 4, 29, 30
'Ringgold' regiment 7
Ropers Church 21, 94

S

Sanson Cutlery Co. 62
Schuylkill County 38
Scott, Ellen Turner xiii
Scranton, Pennsylvania vi, 51, 54, 55, 56, 71, 72, 76, 77, 79, 80, 84, 103, 104, 106
Scranton Republican 71, 104
Scranton Times 72
Seeley, Mrs. 53
Seven Pines, Virginia 16, 21, 23, 94, 95, 96
Shenandoah Valley Campaign v, 29, 30, 31
Sherman, General William Tecumseh ix, 59
Shrewsbury, England 7
Siney, John 44, 50
slave labor 1
slavery 4
Somerdyke, Casper 9, 30
South Carolina 4, 16, 26, 27, 80
St. Aloysius Society 63, 100
State mental hospital, Danville 80
State of Maine 19, 20, 92, 106
steel 2, 3, 39, 41, 80
Stegmaier, George 68
Stephenson, Dr. Benjamin F. 33
St. Helena Island 26, 99
St. James River 24
St. Stephen's Episcopal Church 48, 83
stuffed paddies 24, 97
Susquehanna River 39, 53
Swartzlander, Captain Jacob 8, 32
Sylvis, William H. 38, 104

T

Tamaqua Circle, No. 52, Brotherhood of the Union 45
Thorpe, Jim 43
Titusville, Pennsylvania 5
transcontinental railroad 2, 56
tribes 3
tribulated tanglefoot 18
Tunkhannock, Pennsylvania 53
Turner iii, iv, x, xi, xiii, 12, 74, 103, 104, 106
Turner, Arthur vii
Turner, Arthur H. x
Turner, Donald C. x
Turner, William D. iii, iv, x
Two Weeks Pay Bill 69

U

Union Army iii, 4, 5, 7, 8, 9, 13, 15, 20, 21, 23, 27, 30, 33, 38, 41, 42, 45, 50, 52, 53, 54, 67, 85, 86, 89, 90, 104
Union Army veterans 85
unions xi, 35, 41, 44, 86
United Confederate Veterans 33
Universalist 48
U.S.S. Constitution 19, 92

V

Veterans Administration 81
Veterans of Foreign Wars (VFW) 35
Virginia 2, 3, 4, 5, 16, 19, 20, 29, 103
Volunteer Refreshment Saloon 29

W

Warwick Court House 20, 93
Washington, D.C. vi, 1, 17, 18, 19, 20, 29, 31, 63, 64, 66, 82, 83, 90, 91, 92, 95, 100, 101, 102, 103
When this Cruel War is Over 63
whisky 18
White Oak Swamp 23, 96
Wilkes-Barre Armory 62
Wilkes-Barre Chamber of Commerce 58
Wilkes-Barre & Eastern Railroad 59
Wilkes-Barre, Pennsylvania vi, xiii, 36, 37, 39, 41, 42, 45, 48, 50, 51, 52, 53, 54, 55, 56, 58, 59, 60, 62, 63, 64, 65, 66, 68, 70, 71, 72, 76, 77, 78, 79, 80, 82, 83, 84, 100, 103, 104, 105, 106
Wilkes-Barre Sunday Leader 50, 52
Wilkes-Barre Union Leader 42, 54
Williamsburg 21, 24, 93, 97
Woolson, Albert 33
working conditions xi, 4, 35, 41, 44, 74, 86, 87
Workingman's Benefit Association (WBA) 38
Wright, Honorable J. Ridgway 70
Wyoming Valley 39, 45, 58, 60, 104
Wyoming Valley Sanitarium 45

Y

York River 25, 98
Yorktown 20, 21, 24, 25, 93, 97, 98

www.ingramcontent.com/pod-product-compliance
Lightning Source LLC
Chambersburg PA
CBHW042128100526
44587CB00026B/4208